popina® **book of baking**

popina®
book of baking

Isidora Popović

foreword by Henrietta Green

photography by Peter Cassidy

RYLAND
PETERS
& SMALL

LONDON NEW YORK

**For my parents,
Pavle and Rozalia**

**Design, Photographic Art Direction
and Prop Styling** Steve Painter
Senior Editor Céline Hughes
Production Controller Toby Marshall
Art Director Leslie Harrington
Publishing Director Alison Starling

Food Stylist Linda Tubby
Indexer Hilary Bird

Popina logo and branding Igor Jocić

First published in the UK in 2010
by Ryland Peters & Small
20–21 Jockey's Fields
London WC1R 4BW
www.rylandpeters.com

10 9 8 7 6 5 4 3 2 1

Text © Isidora Popović 2010
Foreword text © Henrietta Green 2010
Design and photographs
© Ryland Peters & Small 2010

Printed in China

ISBN: 978 1 84597 964 5

A CIP record for this book is available from the
British Library.

Notes
• The awards won by Popina for some of their
recipes were bestowed by the Great Taste
Awards, organized by The Guild of Fine Food.
• All spoon measurements are level, unless
otherwise specified.
• All eggs are medium, unless otherwise
specified. It is generally recommended that free-
range eggs be used. Uncooked or partially
cooked eggs should not be served to the very
young, the very old, those with compromised
immune systems, or to pregnant women.
• Ovens should be preheated to the specified
temperature. Recipes in this book were tested
using a fan oven. If using a regular oven, you
may need slightly longer baking times.
• Sterilize preserving jars before use. Wash them
in hot, soapy water and rinse in boiling water.
Place in a large saucepan and then cover with
hot water. With the lid on, bring the water to the
boil and continue boiling for 15 minutes. Turn off
the heat, then leave the jars in the hot water until
just before they are to be filled. Invert the jars
onto clean kitchen paper to dry. Sterilize the lids
for 5 minutes, by boiling, or according to the
manufacturer's instructions. Jars should be filled
and sealed while they are still hot.

contents

foreword

The first time I met Isidora Popović, her bakery business, Popina, had been up and running for no more than a few months. It was a week or two before Christmas and as I strolled down the Portobello Road, I noticed a new stall. Lured by its grace and charm – not something you'd necessarily expect to find in a market in those days – it was filled with different cakes and biscuits wrapped up in cellophane, tied with ribbon and laid out in baskets. Not only did they look gorgeous but yes, they also tasted tantalizing. The quality and generosity of ingredients shone through. A depth of spices or an unusual and arresting blend, a bitingly crisp texture achieved from the simple union of flour and water, or a tender juiciness from the judicious addition of fruits – here was a baker indeed, and with originality, flair and attention to detail. Isidora hovering like a mother hen fussing over her chicks was far too busy to chat and I think I may have disgraced myself that day by trying far too many samples. I just couldn't resist, and coming back for more… and more… but Isidora was far too gracious to comment. Honour was, I hope, restored by the packets I bought for friends and family and of course myself for the coming holidays.

The next time was when I set out to find her at her bakery in London's East End. Isidora had entered a competition for Small Producers and I was the judge. Now if I tell you that over the years I have visited thousands of small producers in their units, you must believe that I am not exaggerating. And so you should also believe me when I tell you meeting Isidora in her 'unit' was like no other. I had no idea that her unit was actually her flat or to be accurate her flat/kitchen/production unit/store room/packing room/office. I have no problem with that (you'd be amazed at some of the places I've visited) but seeing several ovens cramped into a living room and almost every inch used for the storage of tins, trays or some-such baking equipment with Isidora seemingly oblivious to the situation and rising above it all, took my breath away. There she was exuding warmth, passion, total dedication and an obvious hunger for success. Fiercely proud and hugely ambitious, she represented, as she told me without a moment's hesitation 'food artistry from the soul'.

In one way, not much has changed since then. With Isidora at the helm, the quality remains consistent whatever the scale or production or success. I may not bump into Isidora serving at farmers' markets any more but when I bite into one of her products, I think of her and smile. I am delighted that she has succeeded in her stated ambition to deliver to every customer 'the whole experience of taste, texture and the visual' and now there's the added bonus of sharing with home cooks her recipes in this book.

Henrietta Green

introduction

I was born in Serbia, in a town called Novi Sad on the river Danube. In those days there were no big supermarkets in Serbia, so every day my mother went to the market where local farmers, cheesemongers, butchers and fisherman brought their produce grown, made or caught either in surrounding farms or in mountains deeper in the country. She always prepared breakfast, lunch and dinner from scratch using the fresh ingredients she had bought that day. To this day, when I work on a recipe, I keep the picture of this childhood market in my head as a guiding image: the most amazing palette of colours bathed in sunshine, seasonal fruit and vegetables with their inviting smells, the hustle and bustle of market life – a real cornucopia.

I used to love watching my mother cook – she was so inventive with flavours and recipes. In the autumn we picked fruit from which we made jams and compotes; we cooked tomatoes to make and store their sauce; we pickled cabbage, cucumbers and peppers in the colours of the rainbow; we collected and dried nuts; we bought meat to make sausages and cure ham; and we dried flowers and herbs for the winter. Food and cooking weren't merely a necessity, they were a passion and an identity to be passed with pride to the next generations.

I started Popina in 1999 after completing an art degree at Goldsmiths in London. I had just designed an art project based on food and I felt so passionately about food that I wanted to share this and develop my interest. A great opportunity arose when, after a long wait, I got a pitch on Portobello Market in Notting Hill. With financial help and tremendous support from The Prince's Trust, I set up Popina as a business and started trading. The company name was chosen because the word means 'eatery' in Latin and suggests a welcoming place to eat. In true London style, Popina's recipes have always reflected a mixture of cultural influences and culinary inspiration.

In the early days I was baking biscuits at home and bringing them to the busy market to sell. My greatest driving force and encouragement came from my customers, who loved our treats and came religiously to buy them. In its ten years, Popina's recipes have won many prestigious food awards and been enjoyed by food-lovers in the UK and abroad.

Popina is about imagination, seasonality and a love of making great food, simply. My inspiration comes from a respect for nature and the constant need to create, learn and be challenged. This book is a selection of my favourite recipes, some of which were among the first on that market stall ten years ago; others you can still buy today.

I sincerely hope you enjoy making the recipes as much as I did devising them, and I urge you to use this book as a canvas for your own creations.

Isidora Popović

popina
biscuits, biscotti & bites

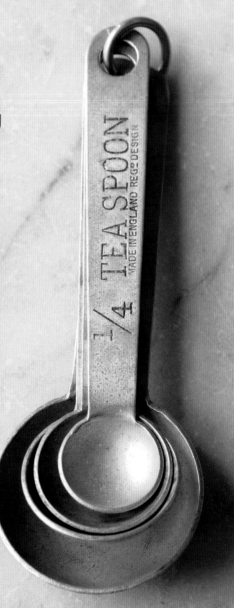

ginger, oat and sultana cookies

Fruity, with warm tones of ginger – best enjoyed warm from the oven.

110 g unsalted butter, at room temperature

145 g light brown soft sugar

1 tablespoon golden syrup

1 egg

200 g plain flour

½ teaspoon baking powder

30 g jumbo oats

70 g crystallized ginger, chopped

70 g sultanas

1–2 baking trays, lined with greaseproof paper

Makes about 12

Cream the butter and sugar in a mixing bowl until light and fluffy. Add the syrup and egg and mix well. Mix the flour, baking powder and oats together in a separate bowl, then mix into the wet ingredients. Finally, mix in the ginger and sultanas.

Roll the dough into a log 5 cm in diameter, wrap in clingfilm and refrigerate for about 1 hour.

Preheat the oven to 170°C (325°F) Gas 3.

Remove the dough from the fridge and unwrap it. Cut into discs about 2 cm thick. Arrange the discs on the prepared baking tray(s), spacing them well apart as they will spread when they are baking.

Bake in the preheated oven for about 20–25 minutes until the cookies are pale gold. Remove from the oven and leave to cool for a few minutes, then serve warm. Store in an airtight container for up to 1 week.

pecan and cranberry cookies

Lovely sweet pecan nuts contrasting with the sharpness of dried cranberries. This is my favourite winter cookie.

110 g unsalted butter, at room temperature

145 g light brown soft sugar

1 tablespoon golden syrup

a few drops of vanilla extract

1 egg

200 g plain flour

½ teaspoon baking powder

30 g shelled pecan nuts, chopped

30 g dried cranberries

1–2 baking trays, lined with greaseproof paper

Makes about 12

Cream the butter and sugar in a mixing bowl until light and fluffy. Add the syrup, vanilla and egg and mix well. Mix the flour and baking powder together in a separate bowl, then mix into the wet ingredients. Finally, mix in the pecans and cranberries.

Roll the dough into a log 5 cm in diameter, wrap in clingfilm and refrigerate for about 1 hour.

Preheat the oven to 170°C (325°F) Gas 3.

Remove the dough from the fridge and unwrap it. Cut into discs about 2 cm thick. Arrange the discs on the prepared baking tray(s), spacing them well apart as they will spread when they are baking.

Bake in the preheated oven for about 20–25 minutes until the cookies are pale gold. Remove from the oven and leave to cool for a few minutes, then serve warm. Store in an airtight container for up to 1 week.

chocolate chip cookies

You can use chocolate chips for these cookies or simply chop up some good chocolate bars. Eat the cookies warm while the chocolate is still molten.

120 g unsalted butter, at room temperature

165 g light brown soft sugar

1 tablespoon golden syrup

a few drops of vanilla extract

1 egg

210 g plain flour

½ teaspoon baking powder

60 g dark chocolate, chopped (or use chips)

60 g milk chocolate, chopped (or use chips)

1–2 baking trays, lined with greaseproof paper

Makes about 12

Cream the butter and sugar in a mixing bowl until light and fluffy. Add the syrup, vanilla and egg and mix well. Mix the flour and baking powder together in a separate bowl, then mix into the wet ingredients. Finally, mix in the chopped chocolate.

Roll the dough into a log 5 cm in diameter, wrap in clingfilm and refrigerate for about 1 hour.

Preheat the oven to 170°C (325°F) Gas 3.

Remove the dough from the fridge and unwrap it. Cut into discs about 2 cm thick. Arrange the discs on the prepared baking tray(s), spacing them well apart as they will spread when they are baking.

Bake in the preheated oven for about 20–25 minutes until the cookies are pale gold. Remove from the oven and leave to cool for a few minutes, then serve warm. Store in an airtight container for up to 1 week.

oat and raisin cookies

A classic cookie made the Popina way – chewy and packed full of oats. Make a few extra dough discs, freeze and save for baking on a lazy weekend afternoon (but leave to thaw for 15 minutes first).

150 g unsalted butter, at room temperature

140 g light brown soft sugar

1 egg

120 g plain flour

½ teaspoon baking powder

½ teaspoon ground cinnamon

80 g jumbo oats

80 g rolled oats

110 g raisins

1–2 baking trays, lined with greaseproof paper

Makes about 12

Cream the butter and sugar in a mixing bowl until light and fluffy. Add the egg and mix well. Mix the flour, baking powder, cinnamon and oats together in a separate bowl, then mix into the wet ingredients. Finally, mix in the raisins.

Roll the dough into a log 5 cm in diameter, wrap in clingfilm and refrigerate for about 1 hour.

Preheat the oven to 170°C (325°F) Gas 3.

Remove the dough from the fridge and unwrap it. Cut into discs about 2 cm thick. Arrange the discs on the prepared baking tray(s), spacing them well apart as they will spread when they are baking.

Bake in the preheated oven for about 20–25 minutes until the cookies are pale gold. Remove from the oven and leave to cool for a few minutes, then serve warm. Store in an airtight container for up to 1 week.

polenta, cherry and nut biscotti

This is an excellent gluten- and dairy-free recipe that I created years ago for my customers on Portobello Road. The biscotti are crumbly, fantastically moreish, and perfect with a strong coffee.

150 g polenta (cornmeal)

70 g rice flour

1½ teaspoons baking powder

100 g golden caster sugar

2 eggs, separated

50 ml apple juice

30 g dried sour cherries (or dried cranberries)

30 g sultanas

30 g shelled pistachio nuts

30 g shelled hazelnuts

a baking tray, lined with greaseproof paper

Makes about 20

Preheat the oven to 150°C (300°F) Gas 2.

Mix the polenta, rice flour, baking powder and sugar.

In a mixing bowl, beat the egg yolks until pale, then add the apple juice and polenta mixture and stir to combine.

In a separate bowl, whisk the egg whites until they form stiff peaks, then gently fold into the polenta mix. Finally, stir in the cherries, sultanas, pistachios and hazelnuts.

Spoon the mixture on to the centre of the prepared baking tray and shape it into a reasonably flat log about 8 cm wide (you can use the greaseproof paper to help you roll the dough).

Bake in the preheated oven for about 30 minutes. To check if it's ready, press very lightly on top of the log and if it springs back you can take it out of the oven. If it still feels very firm, leave it in for a few more minutes.

Using a large, serrated bread knife, slice the log into 1-cm slices. The best way to cut this type of gluten-free pastry is just to press the knife down quickly so that the biscotti doesn't crumble too much.

Lay the slices on the baking tray and return to the hot oven for 10 minutes, turning them halfway through cooking. When they are pale gold, remove from the oven and leave to cool for a few minutes. Store in an airtight container for up to 2 weeks.

fig, apricot and nut biscotti

These double-baked crisp biscuits are packed with dried fruit and nuts, and are made lighter without butter. They are best enjoyed with a cup of strong coffee or dipped in some vanilla ice cream for a sweet treat.

200 g plain flour

1½ teaspoons baking powder

100 g golden caster sugar

30 g shelled pistachio nuts

30 g shelled hazelnuts

30 g sultanas

40 g dried apricots, quartered

40 g dried figs, quartered

freshly grated zest of 1 small unwaxed lemon

2 eggs, lightly beaten

a baking tray, lined with greaseproof paper

Makes about 28

Preheat the oven to 150°C (300°F) Gas 2.

Sift the flour and baking powder into a mixing bowl. Stir in the sugar, pistachio nuts, hazelnuts, sultanas, apricots, figs and lemon zest.

Pour in the eggs and mix well until you get a dough-like mixture. Bring the dough together into a ball in your hands and transfer it to the prepared baking tray.

Flour your hands and roll the dough into a log (you can use the greaseproof paper to help you roll the dough). Flatten it slightly so that it is about 8 cm wide.

Bake in the preheated oven for about 30 minutes. To check if it's ready, press very lightly on top of the log and if it springs back you can take it out of the oven. If it still feels very firm, leave it in the oven for a few more minutes. When it is ready, remove from the oven and leave to cool for about 10 minutes.

Using a large, serrated bread knife, slice the log into 5-mm slices. Lay the slices on the baking tray and return to the hot oven for 10 minutes, turning them halfway through cooking. When they are pale gold, remove from the oven and leave to cool for a few minutes. Store in an airtight container for up to 2 weeks.

white chocolate and fig biscuits

These are super indulgent biscuits – soft, chewy and fruity, with creamy white chocolate chips. Heavenly. Try to buy soft, dried figs as they are the easiest to bake with. If, however, you can only find dried figs, you will have to cut off their hard stalks before you add them to the biscuit dough.

50 g unsalted butter,
at room temperature

80 g golden caster sugar

a few drops of vanilla extract

1 egg

70 g soft, dried figs,
chopped

50 g white chocolate,
chopped (or use chips)

130 g plain flour

1½ teaspoons baking powder

*1–2 baking trays, lined with
greaseproof paper*

Makes about 15

Preheat the oven to 160°C (325°F) Gas 3.

Cream the butter and sugar in a mixing bowl until light and fluffy. Add the vanilla and egg and mix well. Stir in the figs and chopped chocolate. Mix the flour and baking powder together in a separate bowl, then gently fold into the wet ingredients.

Take a generous teaspoon of the biscuit dough and place on one of the prepared baking trays. Flatten slightly, then repeat with the remaining dough, spacing the dough balls well apart as they will spread when they are baking.

Bake in the preheated oven for about 25 minutes, or until the biscuits are pale gold. Remove from the oven and leave to cool for a few minutes. Store in an airtight container for up to 1 week.

ginger and chilli caramel biscuits

These addictive biscuits are drizzled with hot caramel, so you can explore your artistic side when it comes to decorating them! With a generous dose of crystallized ginger and bit of chilli heat, they are not for the faint-hearted.

50 g unsalted butter, at room temperature

100 g golden caster sugar

1 egg

50 g crystallized ginger, finely chopped

130 g plain flour

1½ teaspoons baking powder

2 teaspoons ground ginger

Chilli caramel

100 g golden caster sugar

a pinch of ground cayenne pepper or hot chilli powder (or more if you like the heat!)

1–2 baking trays, lined with greaseproof paper

Makes about 15

Preheat the oven to 160°C (325°F) Gas 3.

Cream the butter and sugar in a mixing bowl until light and fluffy. Add the egg and mix well, then stir in the crystallized ginger. Mix the flour, baking powder and ground ginger in a separate bowl, then gently fold into the wet ingredients.

Take a generous teaspoon of the dough and place on one of the prepared baking trays. Flatten it slightly, then repeat this process with the remaining dough, spacing the dough balls well apart as they will spread when they are baking.

Bake in the preheated oven for about 25 minutes, or until the biscuits are golden. Remove from the oven and leave to cool while you make the chilli caramel.

To make the chilli caramel, put the sugar in a heavy-based saucepan over medium heat. The sugar can burn quite easily (which can render the caramel bitter), so stir it often and keep a close eye on it. After a few minutes, the sugar should have completely melted. Remove from the heat and stir in the pepper or chilli powder. Be very careful when handling caramel as it can easily burn you. Use it immediately before it starts to harden.

Using a spoon, drizzle the caramel over the biscuits any way you like. The caramel sets extremely quickly. When it has set, remove the biscuits from the tray. Store in an airtight container for up to 1 week, but be warned that the caramel can seep into the biscuits in particularly humid conditions.

pineapple, coconut and lemon biscuits

I recommend making the candied pineapple in advance, as it keeps well for weeks and you can use it any time to make a batch of these biscuits. You can also store the cooking syrup, which has a wonderful pineapple flavour and which I use to season my breakfast porridge.

100 g unsalted butter, at room temperature

180 g golden granulated sugar, or 180 g pineapple syrup (see method)

2 eggs

finely grated zest of 1 unwaxed lemon

120 g desiccated coconut or finely grated fresh coconut

260 g plain flour

2 teaspoons baking powder

Candied pineapple

430 g tinned pineapple pieces in juice, drained

500 g golden granulated sugar

2 baking trays, lined with greaseproof paper

Makes about 24

To make the candied pineapple, put the drained pineapple pieces and sugar in a saucepan over low/medium heat. The sugar, along with the natural juices from the pineapple, will form a syrup and the edges of the pineapple will become translucent. Stir occasionally, then take the pan off the heat after 30 minutes – the pineapple pieces will still have a bite to them and will be full of flavour.

Leave to cool for 15 minutes. Pick out the pineapple pieces and chop them up if they are still too big. Use them straight-away or put them in a lidded jar or airtight container along with just a few tablespoons of the syrup. You can also store the syrup in separate jar or container to use another day.

Preheat the oven to 160°C (325°F) Gas 3.

Cream the butter and sugar (or 180 g of the reserved pineapple syrup) in a mixing bowl until light and fluffy. Add the eggs and mix well, then stir in the lemon zest, candied pineapple and coconut. Mix the flour and baking powder in a separate bowl, then gently fold into the wet ingredients.

Take a generous teaspoon of the dough and place on one of the prepared baking trays. Flatten it slightly, then repeat this process with the remaining dough, spacing the dough balls well apart as they will spread when they are baking.

Bake in the preheated oven for about 25 minutes, or until the biscuits are golden. Remove from the oven and leave to cool for a few minutes. Store in an airtight container for up to 1 week.

spelt, chocolate and hazelnut biscuits

I love wholemeal spelt flour and it works incredibly well with this combination of hazelnuts and chocolate.

80 g unsalted butter, at room temperature

110 g golden caster sugar

1 egg

a few drops of vanilla extract

145 g wholemeal spelt flour

1 teaspoon baking powder

40 g shelled hazelnuts, roughly chopped

50 g dark chocolate, chopped (or use chips)

30 g milk chocolate, chopped (or use chips)

1–2 baking trays, lined with greaseproof paper

Makes about 17

Preheat the oven to 160°C (325°F) Gas 3.

Cream the butter and sugar in a mixing bowl until light and fluffy. Add the egg and vanilla and mix well. Mix the flour and baking powder in a separate bowl, then gently fold into the wet ingredients. Finally, mix in the hazelnuts and chopped chocolate.

Take a generous teaspoon of the biscuit dough and place on one of the prepared baking trays. Flatten it slightly, then repeat this process with the remaining dough, spacing the dough balls well apart as they will spread when they are baking.

Bake in the preheated oven for about 25 minutes, or until the biscuits are deep golden. Remove from the oven and leave to cool for a few minutes. Store in an airtight container for up to 1 week.

walnut shortbreads

Crumbly and buttery with a strong taste of walnuts. If you have time, you can very lightly roast the walnuts to give these delightful biscuits that extra punch.

100 g shelled walnuts

90 g unsalted butter, at room temperature

60 g golden caster sugar

a few drops of vanilla extract

125 g plain flour

icing sugar or vanilla sugar, to dust

1–2 baking trays, lined with greaseproof paper

Makes about 16

Preheat the oven to 130°C (250°F) Gas ½.

If you have time, put the walnuts on a baking tray and roast in the preheated oven for 10 minutes, then roughly chop one half and finely chop the other (or blitz in a food processor). If you are short of time, skip this roasting step and just chop the nuts as above.

Cream the butter, sugar and vanilla in a mixing bowl until light and fluffy. Stir in the walnuts, then gently fold in the flour until well mixed.

Roll the dough into a log 3 cm in diameter, then cut into discs about 2 cm thick. Roughly roll each disc into a ball – it should be about the size of a walnut. Arrange the dough balls on the baking tray(s), spacing them well apart as they will spread when they are baking.

Bake in the preheated oven for about 30 minutes – they should still be slightly soft in the middle. Remove from the oven and dust with icing sugar or vanilla sugar. Store in an airtight container for up to 2 weeks.

hazelnut macaroons

This is another dairy- and gluten-free biscuit. If you prefer, you can use ground almonds in place of the rice flour – it will make the macaroons a touch softer. They are crunchy on the outside, chewy in the middle, and very, very nutty.

160 g blanched hazelnuts

2 egg whites

160 g golden caster sugar

40 g rice flour (or ground almonds)

a few drops of vanilla extract

a baking tray, lined with greaseproof paper

Makes about 20

Preheat the oven to 130°C (250°F) Gas ½.

Put the hazelnuts on a baking tray and roast in the preheated oven for about 15 minutes, or until very pale gold. Grind them finely in a spice grinder or food processor, leaving a few chunkier pieces.

In a mixing bowl, mix the egg whites and sugar just to combine, then add the ground hazelnuts, rice flour and vanilla. Cover with clingfilm and refrigerate for 30 minutes.

Take the mixture out of the fridge and stir through with a spoon. Take a generous teaspoon of the dough and place on the prepared baking tray. Flatten it slightly, then repeat this process with the remaining dough, spacing the dough balls slightly apart as they may spread when they are baking.

Bake in the preheated oven for about 25 minutes, or until the macaroons are very pale gold. They should still be slightly soft in the middle. Remove from the oven and leave to cool for a few minutes. Store in an airtight container for up to 1 week.

gingerbread men and women

These are great fun to make with children – they can get creative and dress up the gingerbread people with different types of chocolate, nuts or dried fruit. For a less dressy person, stick to white chocolate.

175 g plain flour

1 teaspoon baking powder

1½ teaspoons ground ginger

80 g unsalted butter, chilled and cubed

40 g golden caster sugar

50 g runny honey

1 teaspoon water

about 50 g white chocolate, melted (or any other chocolate, nuts and dried fruit), to decorate

gingerbread men cutters in sizes of your choice

a baking tray, lined with greaseproof paper

Makes about 4 grown-ups

Preheat the oven to 170°C (325°F) Gas 3.

Put the flour, baking powder, ginger, butter, sugar and honey in a food processor and pulse until you get crumbs. Add the water and mix until a smooth ball of dough has formed.

Transfer the dough to a lightly floured surface and roll out with a rolling pin until about 5 mm thick. Cut out people with your chosen cutters and place on the prepared baking tray.

Bake in the preheated oven for 20–30 minutes, then leave to cool before decorating.

To decorate, pipe molten white chocolate clothes on to the gingerbread people, or accessorize with chopped nuts and dried fruit. Store in an airtight container for up to 2 weeks.

easter egg biscuits

These are great-looking chocolate biscuits studded with dried fruit and nuts. You can decorate them by scattering the nuts and dried fruit over them haphazardly or spend time over an artistic design. Either way, they make thoughtful Easter gifts.

150 g plain flour

1 teaspoon baking powder

15 g cocoa powder

50 g light brown soft sugar

65 g unsalted butter, chilled and cubed

45 g runny honey

1 teaspoon water

To decorate

100 g white chocolate, chopped

30 g shelled almonds, chopped

30 g shelled pistachio nuts, chopped

30 g shelled pecan nuts, chopped (optional)

30 g dried cranberries, chopped

an 11-cm high, egg-shaped biscuit cutter

a baking tray, lined with greaseproof paper

Makes 5

Preheat the oven to 170°C (325°F) Gas 3.

Put the flour, baking powder, cocoa, sugar, butter and honey in a food processor and pulse until you get crumbs. Add the water and mix until a smooth ball of dough has formed.

Transfer the dough to a lightly floured surface and roll out with a rolling pin until about 5 mm thick. Cut out egg shapes with the biscuit cutter and place on the prepared baking tray.

Bake in the preheated oven for 25 minutes, then leave to cool before decorating.

To decorate, put the chocolate in a heatproof bowl over a saucepan of barely simmering water. Do not let the base of the bowl touch the water. Stir until melted.

Brush the melted chocolate over one side of each biscuit with a pastry brush, then scatter the nuts and cranberries over the top. If you prefer, you can arrange the decoration in a pattern.

Leave the chocolate to cool and set before serving. Store in an airtight container away from sunlight for up to 2 weeks.

granola bars

These wholesome, moreish granola bars take almost no time to make and are perfect get-ahead treats for those weekday mornings when you don't have time to make breakfast.

170 g light brown soft sugar

75 g golden syrup

130 g unsalted butter

75 ml apple juice

190 g jumbo oats

190 g rolled oats

95 g sultanas

50 g pumpkin seeds

50 g sunflower seeds

a 20 x 30-cm baking tray or tart tin (3 cm deep), lined with greaseproof paper

Makes 12 large bars

Preheat the oven to 180°C (350°F) Gas 4.

Put the sugar, syrup, butter and apple juice in a saucepan and gently bring to the boil. Remove from the heat and stir in the remaining ingredients until well mixed. Transfer to the prepared tin and spread evenly.

Bake in the preheated oven for 15–20 minutes, then remove from the oven and leave to cool.

Lift the greaseproof paper, granola and all, up and out of the tin, and transfer to a chopping board. Cut into bars and store in an airtight container for up to 1 week.

florentines

These nutty, fruity nibbles dipped in dark chocolate are perfect after-dinner Christmas treats served with coffee or tea. We sell them gift-wrapped for stocking fillers. If you have a mini-muffin tin, you can bake the florentines in this so that you get perfect circles, but it's just as easy to make them by hand and bake them on a tray.

60 g unsalted butter

60 g golden granulated sugar

60 g runny honey

60 g plain flour

35 g mixed peel

35 g dried cranberries

65 g sultanas

45 g flaked almonds, plus extra to sprinkle

35 g shelled walnuts, chopped

35 g shelled pecan nuts, chopped

80 g dark chocolate, chopped

1–2 baking trays, lined with greaseproof paper

Makes about 20

Preheat the oven to 150°C (300°F) Gas 2.

Put the butter, sugar and honey in a saucepan over medium heat and gently bring to the boil. Do not let the ingredients burn. When it reaches boiling point, stir until the sugar has dissolved completely, then remove from the heat.

Stir in the flour, mixed peel, cranberries, sultanas, almonds, walnuts and pecan nuts. Mix until well combined. Leave to cool for a while before handling.

Take a generous teaspoon of the mixture, roughly roll into a ball and place on one of the prepared baking trays. Flatten it gently, then repeat this process with the remaining mixture, spacing the discs apart as they may spread when they are baking. Sprinkle a few flaked almonds over each florentine.

Bake in the preheated oven for 15 minutes. Remove from the oven and leave to cool.

In the meantime, put the chocolate in a heatproof bowl over a saucepan of barely simmering water. Do not let the base of the bowl touch the water. Stir until melted. Dip one side of each florentine in the bowl of melted chocolate and leave to set, chocolate side up, on a cooling rack. Store in an airtight container for up to 2 weeks.

popina
sweet
tarts

pastry bases

These three pastry bases are used, individually or together, in all of Popina's tart recipes. They are so simple that I would encourage you to experiment with different seasonal fruit fillings and make your own masterpiece! If you have any dough left over, freeze it for next time.

sweet shortcrust

250 g plain flour

125 g unsalted butter, chilled and cubed

85 g golden caster sugar

1 egg

Makes enough to line a 23-cm tart tin

Put the flour, butter and sugar in a mixer and blitz until you get crumbs. Add the egg and mix again. Take the dough out of the mixer and bring together into a ball. If you prefer, you can make the dough by hand, but it's easier to do this if the butter is grated or very finely chopped.

Put the dough on a lightly floured surface and roll with a rolling pin until 3–4 mm thick.

Turn to the tart recipe you are using and continue following the instructions.

chocolate shortcrust

225 g plain flour

25 g cocoa powder

125 g unsalted butter, chilled and cubed

85 g golden caster sugar

1 egg

Makes enough to line a 23-cm tart tin

Put the flour, cocoa, butter and sugar in a mixer and blitz until you get crumbs. Add the egg and mix again. Take the dough out of the mixer and bring together into a ball. If you prefer, you can make the dough by hand, but it's easier to do this if the butter is grated or very finely chopped.

Put the dough on a lightly floured surface and roll with a rolling pin until 3–4 mm thick.

Turn to the tart recipe you are using and continue following the instructions.

sponge dough

45 g unsalted butter, at room temperature

90 g golden caster sugar

1 egg

1½ teaspoons baking powder

90 g plain flour

Makes enough to line a 23-cm tart tin

Put the butter and sugar in a mixing bowl and mix with an electric whisk to combine.

Mix in the egg and baking powder with the whisk, then gently fold in the flour by hand until evenly combined.

Turn to the tart recipe you are using and continue following the instructions.

apple and plum tart

An absolutely classic Popina recipe and always on our menu! When we first produced these tarts on our farmers' market stall, we sold hundreds every weekend. I recommend using strongly flavoured, tart apples like Bramley, and a sweet plum variety like Victoria. There is plenty of fruit filling, which makes it wonderfully juicy. Best eaten either warm from the oven or chilled with some custard.

1 Sweet Shortcrust recipe (see page 40)

1 Sponge Dough recipe (see page 40)

2 Bramley apples, cored and cut into 1-cm thick slices

10 Victoria plums, stoned and halved

3 tablespoons apricot jam, to glaze (optional)

a 23-cm loose-based fluted tart tin, greased

Makes about 8 slices

Preheat the oven to 160°C (325°F) Gas 3.

Line the tart tin with the Sweet Shortcrust pastry and trim the excess dough neatly around the edges. Spoon the Sponge Dough into the tart shell and spread evenly. Scatter the apples and plums all over the sponge.

Bake in the preheated oven for 40 minutes. When the tart is ready, the fruit will have sunk a little and the sponge will have risen up in parts and be golden. Remove from the oven and leave to cool for a few minutes.

In the meantime, put the apricot jam, if using, in a small saucepan and heat gently until melted and runny. Brush the jam all over the tart filling with a pastry brush and leave for a few more minutes before serving. Alternatively, serve it straight from the fridge with a helping of custard.

rhubarb custard and crumble tartlets

Creamy rhubarb custard tarts with crumbly butter biscuit on top. If you like, you can skip the crumble step and simply crush 170 g good, shop-bought shortbread instead. For an extra helping of decadence, serve with custard. You can even make more of the mashed rhubarb, then push it through a sieve to make a lovely coulis for pouring on to the tartlet. Using forced rhubarb will make it a fantastic vibrant pink.

1 Sweet Shortcrust recipe
(see page 40)

Crumble

100 g plain flour

50 g unsalted butter,
chilled and cubed

40 g golden caster sugar

Rhubarb custard

360 g rhubarb, trimmed and
chopped into small pieces

130 g golden caster sugar

3 eggs

a few drops of vanilla extract

130 ml double cream

*a baking tray, lined with
greaseproof paper*

*6 x 9-cm loose-based fluted
tartlet tins, greased*

Makes 6

Preheat the oven to 180°C (350°F) Gas 4.

To make the crumble, mix the flour, butter and sugar in a food processor. Bring the dough together with your hands and transfer to a lightly floured surface. Roll with a rolling pin until about 3 mm thick, then place on the prepared baking tray. Bake in the preheated oven for 15 minutes, or until pale gold. Remove from the oven (leaving the oven on) and leave to cool completely, then crush into crumbs and set aside.

Line the tartlet tins with the Sweet Shortcrust pastry and trim the excess dough neatly around the edges. Blind bake for 10 minutes, or until pale gold. Leave the oven on.

To make the rhubarb custard, put the rhubarb in a roasting tray, sprinkle over the sugar and give it a stir. Cover with foil and roast in the hot oven for about 20–25 minutes, until soft. Remove from the oven, leave to cool for a few minutes, then blitz roughly in a food processor or mash with a fork.

Reduce the oven temperature to 150°C (300°F) Gas 2.

Whisk the eggs and vanilla together. Pour the cream into a saucepan over low heat and gently bring to the boil, stirring frequently. Remove from the heat and whisk in the eggs and vanilla and then the rhubarb until well combined.

Fill each tartlet shell up to the top with rhubarb custard and bake in the hot oven for 15–20 minutes, until the filling no longer wobbles when you shake the tartlet. Remove from the oven and scatter crumble over the top. Leave to cool slightly before serving or even better, serve chilled.

fig, grape and frangipane tartlets

The best time to make these is late summer to early autumn when figs are in season and at their most flavoursome. If you can also get hold of black Muscat grapes, you'll have a rhapsody of flavours!

1 Sweet Shortcrust recipe (see page 40)

50 g unsalted butter, at room temperature

50 g golden caster sugar

1 large egg

50 g ground almonds

50 g plain flour

4 drops of almond extract

6 fresh figs, halved and stalks slightly trimmed

about 24 red (or black Muscat) grapes

6 x 10-cm loose-based fluted tartlet tins, greased

Makes 6

Preheat the oven to 160°C (325°F) Gas 3.

Line the tartlet tins with the Sweet Shortcrust pastry and trim the excess dough neatly around the edges. Refrigerate while you make the filling.

Put the butter, sugar, egg, ground almonds, flour and almond extract in a food processor and mix until you get a soft cream.

Fill each tartlet shell up to the top with almond cream and spread evenly, then arrange 2 fig halves and about 4 grapes on top. Bake in the preheated oven for about 20–25 minutes. When the tartlets are ready, the almond cream will be golden. Remove from the oven and leave to cool for a few minutes.

nectarine and summer berry tart

This is my favourite summer tart – it's bursting with all kinds of berries, plus nectarines, which make everything taste extra summery! I would encourage you, whenever possible, to buy your fruit directly from your local farmers' market where the growers bring them in season and when they are ripe and full of flavour.

1 Sweet Shortcrust recipe
(see page 40)

1 Sponge Dough recipe
(see page 40)

200 g nectarines, stoned
and sliced

a handful of blueberries

a handful of raspberries

a handful of strawberries,
hulled and halved

3 tablespoons apricot jam,
to glaze (optional)

*a 23-cm loose-based fluted
tart tin, greased*

Makes about 8 slices

Preheat the oven to 160°C (325°F) Gas 3.

Line the tart tin with the Sweet Shortcrust pastry and trim the excess dough neatly around the edges. Spoon the Sponge Dough into the tart shell and spread evenly. Scatter the nectarines, then the berries all over the sponge.

Bake in the preheated oven for 40 minutes. When the tart is ready, the fruit will have sunk a little and the sponge will have risen up in parts and be golden. Remove from the oven and leave to cool for a few minutes.

Put the apricot jam, if using, in a small saucepan and heat gently until melted and runny. Brush the jam all over the tart filling with a pastry brush and leave for a few more minutes before serving with a dollop of crème fraîche.

rustic plum tart

This recipe was created with late summer in mind. It's very simple, light and fruity, and really you can make it with any ripe fruit you have a glut of. A variation that works particularly well, though, is apple and cinnamon, which is the winter partner to the summer plum.

90 g golden caster sugar

1 egg

40 ml groundnut oil (or any vegetable oil)

55 ml whole milk

140 g plain flour

1 teaspoon baking powder

a few drops of vanilla extract

6 large plums, stoned and halved

2 tablespoons apricot jam, to glaze (optional)

a 20-cm springform tin, lined with greaseproof paper

Makes about 6 slices

Preheat the oven to 180°C (350°F) Gas 4.

Put the sugar and egg in a mixing bowl and mix with an electric whisk. Add the oil, milk, flour, baking powder and vanilla and mix again until combined. Transfer to the prepared baking tin and spread evenly. Sit the plums, cut side up, over the mixture.

Bake in the preheated oven for about 30 minutes, or until deep golden. Remove from the oven and leave to cool for a few minutes.

In the meantime, put the apricot jam, if using, in a small saucepan and heat gently until melted and runny. Brush the jam all over the tart with a pastry brush and leave for a few more minutes before serving.

Variation: Substitute ½ teaspoon ground cinnamon for the vanilla extract, and 1 Bramley apple, cored and sliced, for the plums. Follow the recipe as above.

chocolate and pistachio tartlets

This recipe is made in two parts and there is something incredibly satisfying about covering the chocolate sponge in the rich ganache. I recommend that you use good-quality dark chocolate, at least 70% cocoa solids if possible. The variation at the bottom of the page is for creamy white chocolate ganache tartlets with just a hint of coffee.

1 Chocolate Shortcrust recipe, or plain Sweet Shortcrust if you prefer (see page 40)

a handful of shelled pistachio nuts, chopped, to decorate

Chocolate sponge

70 g golden caster sugar

1 egg

55 g plain flour

½ teaspoon baking powder

2 teaspoons cocoa powder

10 g unsalted butter

35 g dark chocolate, chopped

2 tablespoons water

Chocolate ganache

50 g dark chocolate, finely chopped

50 g milk chocolate, finely chopped

150 ml double cream

6 x 9-cm loose-based fluted tartlet tins, greased

Makes 6

Preheat the oven to 180°C (350°F) Gas 4.

Line the tartlet tins with the Chocolate Shortcrust pastry and trim the excess dough neatly around the edges. Refrigerate while you make the filling.

To make the chocolate sponge, put the sugar and egg in a mixing bowl and beat with an electric whisk until pale yellow. Gently fold in the flour, baking powder and cocoa powder. In a heatproof bowl, melt the butter and chocolate over a pan of simmering water, then add to the mixing bowl. Add the water and mix well.

Spoon about 1½ tablespoons chocolate sponge into each tartlet shell. Bake in the preheated oven for 15 minutes. Remove from the oven and leave to cool for 10 minutes.

To make the chocolate ganache, put the chocolate in a mixing bowl. Put the cream in a saucepan and gently bring to the boil over low heat, stirring frequently. Pour into the mixing bowl and whisk until you get a smooth cream.

Pour the chocolate ganache into the tartlets, then scatter the pistachio nuts over the top. Refrigerate and serve chilled.

Variation: To make White Mocha Tartlets, the instructions are as above but you need to add 1 teaspoon instant coffee to the 2 tablespoons water (hot) in the Chocolate Sponge. You will need to make a White Chocolate Ganache: dissolve ½ teaspoon instant coffee in 1 tablespoon hot water and put in a mixing bowl with 115 g finely chopped white chocolate. Heat 115 ml double cream and gently bring to the boil, then pour into the mixing bowl and whisk until smooth.

chocolate and chestnut tart

Creamy, rich chestnuts paired with a double helping of chocolate –
what more can you ask for in a decadent dessert!

1 Chocolate Shortcrust
recipe (see page 40)

Chestnut sponge

35 g unsalted butter,
at room temperature

35 g golden caster sugar

1 egg

60 g plain flour

1 teaspoon baking powder

30 g cooked chestnuts,
chopped

35 ml double cream, chilled

2 tablespoons cold water

90 g tinned sweetened
chestnut purée

Chocolate ganache

50 g milk chocolate,
finely chopped

50 g dark chocolate,
finely chopped

190 ml double cream

*a 23-cm loose-based fluted
tart tin, greased*

Makes about 8 slices

Preheat the oven to 180°C (350°F) Gas 4.

Line the tart tin with the Chocolate Shortcrust pastry and
trim the excess dough neatly around the edges. Refrigerate
while you make the filling.

To make the chestnut sponge, cream the butter and sugar in
a mixing bowl until light and fluffy. Add the egg and mix well.
Mix the flour, baking powder and chestnuts together in a
separate bowl, then mix into the wet ingredients. Finally,
slowly add the cream and water and incorporate well.

Remove the tart shell from the fridge and spread the
chestnut purée over the base. Spoon the chestnut sponge
on top and spread evenly. Bake in the preheated oven for
20 minutes, or until the dough has risen and is pale gold.
Remove from the oven and leave to cool for a few minutes.
Trim the top of the sponge if it has risen too much.

To make the chocolate ganache, put the chocolate in a
mixing bowl. Put the cream in a saucepan and gently bring
to the boil over low heat, stirring frequently. Pour into the
mixing bowl and whisk until you get a smooth cream. Leave
to cool for 10 minutes, then pour it into the tart. Refrigerate
and serve chilled.

chocolate, pear and hazelnut tart

This stunning dessert is fit for your most discerning dinner guests, but it is also simple enough to make for a sophisticated picnic.

1 Chocolate Shortcrust recipe (see page 40)

1 Sponge Dough recipe (see page 40)

1 large pear, peeled, halved and cored

20 g shelled hazelnuts (blanched if you like), roughly chopped

2 tablespoons apricot jam (optional)

Chocolate and hazelnut cream

90 g dark chocolate, finely chopped

90 g milk chocolate, finely chopped

180 ml single cream

40 g shelled hazelnuts, roughly chopped and lightly toasted in a dry frying pan

a 23-cm loose-based fluted tart tin, greased

Makes 8–12 slices

Preheat the oven to 170°C (325°F) Gas 3.

Line the tart tin with the Chocolate Shortcrust pastry and trim the excess dough neatly around the edges. Refrigerate while you make the filling.

To make the chocolate and hazelnut cream, put the chocolate in a mixing bowl. Put the cream in a saucepan and gently bring to the boil over low heat, stirring frequently. Pour into the mixing bowl and whisk until you get a smooth cream, then stir in the hazelnuts. Gently fold the Sponge Dough into the chocolate mixture and mix well. Remove the tart shell from the fridge and pour in the chocolate and hazelnut cream.

Cut the pear into about 12 slim wedges and arrange in a circle on top of the tart filling. Sprinkle the hazelnuts over the top. Bake in the preheated oven for about 25 minutes. To check if it's ready, insert a skewer into the centre of the tart – if it comes out clean you can take it out of the oven. If not, leave it in the oven for a few more minutes.

Put the apricot jam, if using, in a small saucepan and heat gently until melted and runny. Brush the jam roughly over the tart (avoiding the hazelnuts) with a pastry brush and leave for a few more minutes before serving.

pecan and bourbon tartlets

Nutty, with the subtle flavour of Bourbon coming through, these smart, irresistible little tarts are perfect for winter entertaining. Bake a batch at Christmastime to round off a festive feast.

1 Sweet Shortcrust recipe (see page 40)

18 pecan halves, to decorate

Date sponge

60 g Medjool dates, stoned (or any soft date)

30 ml double cream

1 tablespoon water

30 g unsalted butter, melted

30 g light brown soft sugar

1 egg

a few drops of vanilla extract

55 g plain flour

1 teaspoon baking powder

Pecan Bourbon filling

1 tablespoon Bourbon whiskey

40 g light brown soft sugar

55 ml golden syrup

1 egg, beaten

20 g unsalted butter, melted

60 g shelled pecan nuts, roughly chopped

6 x 9-cm loose-based fluted tartlet tins, greased

Makes 6

Preheat the oven to 180°C (350°F) Gas 4.

Line the tartlet tins with the Sweet Shortcrust pastry and trim the excess dough neatly around the edges. Refrigerate while you make the filling.

To make date sponge, blitz the dates to a paste in a food processor or simply chop them very finely. Mix with the cream and water and set aside.

Put the butter and sugar in a mixing bowl and mix well, then add the egg, vanilla, flour and baking powder. Finally, add date mixture and fold in well.

Remove the tartlet shells from the fridge and spoon about 1½ tablespoons of the date sponge into them. Bake in the preheated oven for 15 minutes, then remove from the oven (leaving the oven on).

In the meantime, make the pecan Bourbon filling. Put the Bourbon, sugar and syrup in a mixing bowl and mix well. Add the egg, mix well, then stir in the melted butter and pecan nuts.

Spoon the pecan Bourbon filling on top of the tartlets and spread evenly. Decorate with 3 pecan halves and return to the oven for another 10 minutes. Remove from the oven and leave to cool before serving.

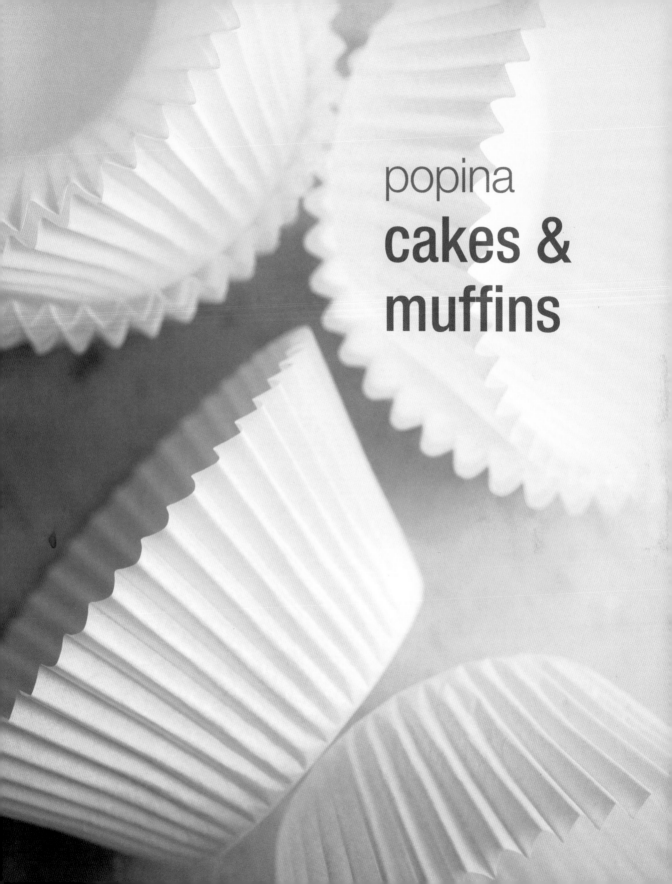

popina
cakes &
muffins

very chocolate cake

This is a seriously rich and creamy gluten-free cake created especially for chocoholics. Use good chocolate with at least 70% cocoa solids.

275 g dark chocolate, chopped

100 g unsalted butter

2 eggs

130 g golden caster sugar

50 g rice flour

1½ teaspoons baking powder

65 ml whole milk

Chocolate icing

140 g unsalted butter, at room temperature

170 g icing sugar

290 g cream cheese

1 tablespoon cocoa powder

a 20-cm springform tin, lined with greaseproof paper

Makes 10–12 slices

Preheat the oven to 160°C (325°F) Gas 3.

Put the chocolate and butter in a heatproof bowl over a saucepan of barely simmering water. Do not let the base of the bowl touch the water. Stir until melted, then leave to cool slightly before using.

Put the eggs and sugar in a mixing bowl and whisk until they have formed a thick foam. Add the rice flour and baking powder and mix, then stir in the melted chocolate and butter. Finally, gently stir in the milk. Pour into the prepared baking tin and bake in the preheated oven for 40 minutes. To check if it's ready, insert a skewer into the centre of the cake – if it comes out clean you can take it out of the oven. If not, leave it in the oven for a few more minutes. Leave the cake to cool completely before turning out of the tin.

In the meantime, make the chocolate icing. Put the butter, sugar, cream cheese and cocoa powder in a food processor and blitz until smooth. Alternatively, put the ingredients in a mixing bowl and whip by hand until smooth. Spread the icing over the cake with a palette knife.

popina carrot cake

This exceptionally light and moist gluten- and dairy-free carrot cake was mastered with love by Popina's own Matt Gruninger.

5 eggs, separated

finely grated zest and freshly squeezed juice of 2 unwaxed lemons

25 ml Kirsch (optional)

250 g golden caster sugar

250 g carrots, grated

250 g ground hazelnuts

2 teaspoons baking powder

65 g cornflour

Lemon icing

300 g icing sugar

freshly squeezed juice of 3 lemons (plus a little grated zest, to decorate)

a 24-cm springform tin, lined with greaseproof paper

Makes about 12 slices

Preheat the oven to 180°C (350°F) Gas 4.

Put the egg yolks, lemon zest and juice, Kirsch (if using), sugar, carrots, hazelnuts and baking powder in a mixing bowl and whisk to combine. Sift in the cornflour and fold it in gently.

In a separate, grease-free bowl, whisk the egg whites until stiff peaks form. Fold the egg whites into the cake mix very gently, then transfer the batter to the prepared baking tin. Bake in the preheated oven for 45 minutes, or until springy in the touch. To check if it's ready, insert a skewer into the centre of the cake – if it comes out clean you can take it out of the oven. If not, leave it in the oven for a few more minutes. Leave the cake to cool completely before turning out of the tin.

In the meantime, make the lemon icing. Mix the sugar and lemon juice well to achieve a runny icing. Remove the cold cake from the tin and pour the icing over it, letting it drip down the sides. Sprinkle with lemon zest.

The cake improves in flavour over a couple of days.

lemon loaf with white chocolate icing

The rich, citrussy base and creamy white chocolate icing are fabulously matched in this perfect teatime cake.

65 g unsalted butter, at room temperature

135 g golden caster sugar

2 eggs

135 g plain flour

1½ teaspoons baking powder

finely grated zest and freshly squeezed juice of 2 unwaxed lemons

White chocolate icing

150 g white chocolate, chopped, plus extra, grated, to decorate

75 ml double cream

a non-stick 2-lb. (17 x 9-cm) loaf tin, lined with greaseproof paper

Makes about 6 slices

Preheat the oven to 170°C (325°F) Gas 3.

Put the butter and sugar in a mixing bowl and mix well with an electric whisk. Add the eggs and whisk for a couple of minutes until pale and fluffy. Gently fold in the flour and baking powder. Finally, stir in the lemon zest and juice until well mixed.

Pour the mixture into the prepared loaf tin and bake in the preheated oven for 25 minutes. When it's ready, the cake will be a rich golden colour and springy to the touch. Remove it from the oven and leave to cool before icing.

In the meantime, make the white chocolate icing. Put the chocolate in a mixing bowl. Put the cream in a saucepan and gently bring to the boil over low heat, stirring frequently. Pour into the mixing bowl and whisk until you get a smooth cream. Leave to cool for a couple of minutes, then refrigerate for 15 minutes to stiffen.

Spread the icing on top of the cake and sprinkle some grated chocolate over it.

cranberry, sherry and vine fruit cake

We serve this cake as an alternative to traditional Christmas cake. It is loaded with sherry-soaked fruits, walnuts and cranberries.

60 g unsalted butter, at room temperature

50 g light brown soft sugar

1 tablespoon molasses (or black treacle)

2 small eggs, beaten

60 g plain flour

1½ teaspoons baking powder

½ teaspoon ground cinnamon

freshly grated zest of 1 unwaxed orange

50 g fresh or frozen cranberries

20 g shelled walnuts, chopped

Sherry-soaked fruits

100 g raisins

130 g sultanas

60 g mixed peel

3 tablespoons sherry (dry, if possible)

40 ml apple juice

Topping

100 g apricot jam

100 g fresh or frozen cranberries

80 g walnut halves

a 20-cm non-stick springform tin

Makes 10–12 slices

Prepare the sherry-soaked fruits at least 24 hours in advance. Put the raisins, sultanas, mixed peel, sherry and apple juice in a bowl. Mix, cover and leave to rest for at least 24 hours.

When you are ready to make the cake, preheat the oven to 180°C (350°F) Gas 4.

Put the butter, sugar and molasses in a mixing bowl and mix well. Fold in the eggs, then add the flour, baking powder, cinnamon, orange zest, cranberries and walnuts. Finally, fold in about 190 g of the soaked fruit, setting the rest aside for the topping. Pour the mixture into the prepared baking tin and bake in the preheated oven for 30 minutes, or until deep golden and springy to the touch. Remove from the oven and leave to cool in the tin.

To make the topping, put the apricot jam in a saucepan and gently bring to the boil over low heat, stirring frequently. Add the cranberries and cook for a few minutes, until their skins just begin to crack. Remove from the heat and stir in the walnuts and the remaining sherry soaked fruits. Mix well and spoon on top of the cake. Cover the cake evenly and press very slightly to fix it in place. Leave to rest for a few hours before serving.

stollen

This is a labour-intensive but rewarding traditional Christmas sweet filled with rum-soaked fruits and plenty of marzipan.

finely grated zest of
1 unwaxed lemon

250 g marzipan

1 egg, beaten

100 g unsalted butter, melted

150 g icing sugar

Rum-soaked fruits

250 g sultanas

170 g mixed peel

80 ml dark or golden rum

Stollen dough

3 teaspoons dried quick yeast

70 g golden caster sugar

140 ml whole milk, warmed

1 large egg yolk

175 g unsalted butter, at room temperature

500 g strong flour

a baking tray, lined with greaseproof paper

Makes 2 stollen

Prepare the rum-soaked fruits at least 24 hours in advance. Put the sultanas, mixed peel and rum in a bowl. Mix, cover and leave to rest for at least 24 hours.

When you are ready to make the stollen dough, stir the yeast and sugar into the warm milk and set aside for 5 minutes.

Put the egg yolk, butter and flour in a mixing bowl and add the yeast mixture. Mix until you get a smooth dough, then transfer to a lightly floured surface and knead for 5 minutes. The dough should be soft but not sticky. If it is sticky, add a little flour and knead again. Return the dough to the mixing bowl, dust in flour, cover and leave to prove for 1 hour in a warm place. The dough should increase significantly in size.

Stir the lemon zest into the rum-soaked fruits, then uncover your mixing bowl and pour in the soaked fruits. Knead the dough again to incorporate and evenly distribute the fruits. Divide the dough in two, cover, and leave to prove for another 40 minutes in a warm place.

Take one ball of dough and roll it out with a rolling pin into a rough square about 5 mm thick. Take half the marzipan and roll it into a tube slightly shorter than the square of dough. Place it along one side of the dough and start to roll the dough up from that side. Keep the sides tucked in as you roll. Repeat with the other ball of dough and remaining marzipan. Brush the beaten egg over the stollen. Cover and leave to prove for another 30 minutes in a warm place.

Preheat the oven to 200°C (400°F) Gas 6.

Put the logs on the prepared baking tray and bake in the preheated oven for 10 minutes, then reduce the heat to 190°C (375°F) Gas 5 and bake for another 20 minutes. Remove from the oven and brush the stollen generously with melted butter. Dust with icing sugar and leave to cool.

chocolate and hazelnut strudel

This is my version of the traditional strudel made with a rich, buttery yeast dough and the strong flour used for making bread. I recommend toasting the hazelnuts lightly, which will give it a stronger nutty flavour.

Strudel dough

1½ teaspoons dried quick yeast

75 ml whole milk, warmed

40 ml warm water

60 g unsalted butter, at room temperature

1 egg yolk

70 g golden caster sugar

a few drops of vanilla extract

2 teaspoons cocoa powder

240 g strong flour

Hazelnut filling

120 g shelled hazelnuts, lightly toasted in a dry frying pan

45 g shelled almonds

130 g icing sugar, plus extra to dust

50 ml water

2 drops of vanilla extract

a baking tray, lined with greaseproof paper

Makes about 10 slices

To make the strudel dough, put the yeast in a jug, then slowly whisk in the warm milk and water and set aside for 5 minutes. Don't worry if it looks like it's curdling.

Cream the butter, egg yolk, sugar, vanilla and cocoa powder in a mixing bowl until light and fluffy. Add the flour and yeast mixture and mix in by hand until you get a smooth dough. Transfer to a well floured surface and knead for a couple of minutes. The dough should be soft but not sticky. If it is sticky, add a little flour and knead again. Return the dough to the mixing bowl, cover and leave to prove for 1½ hours in a warm place. The dough should increase in size.

In the meantime, make the hazelnut filling. Put all the ingredients in a food processor and blitz until you have a loose paste.

Uncover your mixing bowl and transfer the ball of dough to the well floured surface. (You may find it helpful to roll the dough directly on a sheet of greaseproof paper, which will make rolling up the strudel easier.) Knead for a couple of minutes, then roll out with a rolling pin to a rectangle about 35 x 30 cm and 5 mm thick.

Spread the hazelnut filling over the dough with a palette knife, leaving a 2-cm border around the sides and back edge. Start rolling the strudel from the front. The dough will be soft but it should be quite elastic. Do not press or roll the dough too tightly, as it will need some give to expand while baking. Press the ends to seal and fold them underneath the strudel. Transfer to the prepared baking tray, seam side down. Leave to prove for another hour.

Preheat the oven to 200°C (400°F) Gas 6.

Bake the strudel in the preheated oven for 10 minutes, then reduce the heat to 180°C (350°F) Gas 4 and bake for another 15–20 minutes. The strudel should be springy to the touch. Leave to cool, then dust with icing sugar.

poppyseed strudel

If you go anywhere in Eastern Europe, you will come across this cake in one form or another. It is delicious eaten with a glass of cold milk.

Strudel dough

1½ teaspoons dried quick yeast

60 ml whole milk, warmed

3 tablespoons warm water

215 g strong flour

75 g unsalted butter, at room temperature

1 egg yolk

45 g golden caster sugar

Poppyseed filling

100 g poppyseeds

100 g icing sugar

3 tablespoons water

a baking tray, lined with greaseproof paper

Makes about 8–10 slices

To make the strudel dough, put the yeast in a jug, then slowly whisk in the warm milk and water and set aside for 5 minutes. Don't worry if it looks like it's curdling.

Put the flour, butter, egg yolk and sugar in a mixing bowl and mix well. Add the yeast mixture and mix with your hands until you get a smooth dough. Transfer to a well floured surface and knead for a couple of minutes. The dough should be soft but not sticky. If it is sticky, add a little flour and knead again. Return the dough to the mixing bowl, cover and leave to prove for 1 hour in a warm place. The dough should increase significantly in size.

Turn the risen dough out on to the floured surface and knead again for 5 minutes, then leave to rest while you make the filling.

To make the poppyseed filling, put all the ingredients in a coffee or spice grinder and blitz until you have a loose paste.

Transfer the rested dough to the floured surface again. (You may find it helpful to roll the dough directly on a sheet of greaseproof paper, which will make rolling up the strudel easier.) Roll it out with a rolling pin to a square about 25 x 25 cm and 5 mm thick.

Spread the poppyseed filling over the dough with a palette knife, leaving a 2-cm border around the sides and back edge. Start rolling the strudel from the front. The dough will be soft but it should be quite elastic. Do not press or roll the dough too tightly, as it will need some give to expand while baking. Press the ends to seal and fold them underneath the strudel. Transfer to the prepared baking tray, seam side down. Leave to prove for a further 45 minutes.

Preheat the oven to 180°C (350°F) Gas 4.

Bake the strudel in the preheated oven for 25–30 minutes. The strudel should be springy to the touch and be a deep golden colour.

pumpkin and cinnamon filo strudel

Here's the perfect recipe for early autumn – a crumbly, heavenly filo strudel made with creamy, sweet pumpkin and a hint of cinnamon. I make this with large sheets of filo pastry, which I find in Middle Eastern shops or the freezer aisle of my local supermarket. I just let it defrost for 1 hour before I start. If you can't find such large sheets, simply overlap your sheets to make the correct size and remember that you'll need more to begin with.

200 g pumpkin

½ teaspoon ground cinnamon

50 g golden caster sugar

20 ml vegetable oil

3 large sheets of thick filo pastry (47 x 32 cm)

icing sugar, to dust

a baking tray, greased

Makes 6 slices

Preheat the oven to 170°C (325°F) Gas 3.

Peel and deseed the pumpkin, then grate the flesh and squeeze out any excess water. Put in a bowl and mix with the cinnamon and sugar.

Take one sheet of filo pastry, lay it on the prepared baking tray and lightly brush with oil. Place a second sheet on top and lightly brush with oil. Repeat with the third sheet.

Spoon the pumpkin filling along one longer side of the filo sheets, leaving a 2-cm gap on either side and spreading the filling about 5 cm wide. Fold the longer side of the pastry, nearest the filling, about 2 cm in, then roll the filo pastry up, tucking in the sides as you go. When the strudel is baking, the filling will soften and some juice might seep out, so tucking in the sides ensures that not too much juice is lost.

Brush the top of the strudel with a little more oil and bake in the preheated oven for 25 minutes. The strudel should be pale gold. Remove from the oven and leave to cool for 5 minutes. Dust liberally with icing sugar and serve warm.

summer fruit and white chocolate muffins

These are very moist muffins packed full of fruit and nuggets of white chocolate. An indulgent treat with a mid-morning coffee.

2 eggs

80 g golden caster sugar

50 ml vegetable oil (or groundnut or sunflower)

a few drops of vanilla extract

150 g plain flour

1½ teaspoons baking powder

1 large nectarine, stoned and sliced

70 g strawberries, hulled and quartered

70 g white chocolate, chopped

Topping

30 g nectarine, stoned and sliced

60 g raspberries

30 g strawberries, hulled and quartered

light brown soft sugar, to sprinkle

a muffin tray, lined with 6 large muffin cases

Makes 6

Preheat the oven to 180°C (350°F) Gas 4.

Put the eggs, sugar, oil and vanilla in a mixing bowl and mix well until you have a smooth liquid. Mix the flour and baking powder together in a separate bowl, then mix into the wet ingredients. Stir in the nectarines, strawberries and white chocolate until evenly mixed.

Fill each muffin case about two-thirds full with batter. Scatter the fruit for the topping over the muffins and finish with a sprinkling of sugar. Bake in the preheated oven for about 25 minutes. Do not be tempted to open the oven door halfway through baking as it might cause the muffins to sink. When they are ready, they should be well risen and springy to the touch.

Muffins are always best eaten warm from the oven, but if you have some left over you can refresh them with a quick flash in the microwave. Store in an airtight container for 2–3 days.

wholemeal spelt, carrot, apple and pumpkin seed muffins

I love these wholemeal spelt muffins – light, nutty and wholesome with hints of cinnamon and apple.

2 eggs

80 g golden caster sugar

50 ml vegetable oil (or groundnut or sunflower)

150 g wholemeal spelt flour

1½ teaspoons baking powder

1 teaspoon ground cinnamon

1 small carrot, grated

1 small apple, peeled, cored and diced

20 g pumpkin seeds

Topping

30 g pumpkin seeds

light brown soft sugar, to sprinkle

a muffin tray, lined with 6 large muffin cases

Makes 6

Preheat the oven to 180°C (350°F) Gas 4.

Put the eggs, sugar and oil in a mixing bowl and mix well until you have a smooth liquid. Mix the flour, baking powder and cinnamon together in a separate bowl, then mix into the wet ingredients. Stir in the carrot, apple and pumpkin seeds until evenly mixed.

Fill each muffin case about two-thirds full with batter. Scatter the pumpkin seeds for the topping over the muffins and finish with a sprinkling of sugar. Bake in the preheated oven for about 25 minutes. Do not be tempted to open the oven door halfway through baking as it might cause the muffins to sink. When they are ready, they should be well risen and springy to the touch.

Muffins are always best eaten warm from the oven, but if you have some left over you can refresh them with a quick flash in the microwave. Store in airtight container for 2–3 days.

cranberry, orange and pistachio muffins

These muffins look so appealing when you pull them out of the oven on a cold winter's morning. The tart tang of the cranberries ensures that the muffins are not too sweet.

2 eggs

80 g golden caster sugar

50 ml vegetable oil (or groundnut or sunflower)

finely grated zest and freshly squeezed juice of 1 unwaxed orange

150 g plain flour

2½ teaspoons baking powder

100 g fresh or frozen cranberries

Topping

50 g fresh or frozen cranberries

a handful of shelled pistachio nuts, chopped

light brown soft sugar, to sprinkle

a muffin tray, lined with 6 large muffin cases

Makes 6

Preheat the oven to 180°C (350°F) Gas 4.

Put the eggs, sugar, oil, orange zest and juice in a mixing bowl and mix well until you have a smooth liquid. Mix the flour and baking powder together in a separate bowl, then mix into the wet ingredients. Stir in the cranberries until evenly mixed.

Fill each muffin case about two-thirds full with batter. Scatter the cranberries and pistachio nuts for the topping over the muffins and finish with a sprinkling of sugar. Bake in the preheated oven for about 25 minutes. Do not be tempted to open the oven door halfway through baking as it might cause the muffins to sink. When they are ready, they should be well risen and springy to the touch.

Muffins are always best eaten warm from the oven, but if you have some left over you can refresh them with a quick flash in the microwave. Store in airtight container for 2–3 days.

chocolate truffle brownies

This is our Gold Award-winning brownie – soft and creamy, made with the best dark chocolate, and with a similar texture to truffles. Irresistible.

240 g dark chocolate
(at least 70% cocoa solids)

100 g unsalted butter

3 eggs

135 g golden caster sugar

55 g plain flour

cocoa powder, to dust

*an 18-cm square brownie tin
(3 cm deep), lined with
greaseproof paper*

Makes about 9 squares

Preheat the oven to 150°C (300°F) Gas 2.

Put the chocolate and butter in a heatproof bowl over a saucepan of barely simmering water. Do not let the base of the bowl touch the water. Stir until melted. Set aside to cool.

Put the eggs and sugar in a mixing bowl and whisk until pale and creamy. Sift in the flour and fold in gently. Finally, fold in the molten chocolate and mix until smooth.

Pour the batter into the prepared brownie tin and bake in the preheated oven for 15 minutes. The brownies should have risen slightly.

Leave to cool completely, then dust with cocoa powder. Cut into 9 squares and serve.

cherry chocolate truffle brownies

Go the extra mile on these decadent brownies and soak the dried cherries in rum or whisky overnight before starting.

240 g dark chocolate
(at least 70% cocoa solids)

100 g unsalted butter

3 eggs

135 g golden caster sugar

55 g plain flour

30 g dried sour cherries

cocoa powder, to dust

an 18-cm square brownie tin (3 cm deep), lined with greaseproof paper

Makes about 9 squares

Preheat the oven to 150°C (300°F) Gas 2.

Put the chocolate and butter in a heatproof bowl over a saucepan of barely simmering water. Do not let the base of the bowl touch the water. Stir until melted. Set aside to cool.

Put the eggs and sugar in a mixing bowl and whisk until pale and creamy. Sift in the flour and fold in gently. Fold in the molten chocolate and mix until smooth. Stir in the cherries. Pour into the prepared tin and bake in the preheated oven for 15 minutes, or until slightly risen.

Leave to cool. Dust with cocoa and cut into 9 squares.

double orange truffle brownies

A classic combination for those who love mixing orange with chocolate, with mixed peel and natural orange oil.

240 g dark chocolate
(at least 70% cocoa solids)

100 g unsalted butter

3 eggs

135 g golden caster sugar

55 g plain flour

20 g mixed peel

3 drops of natural orange oil

cocoa powder, to dust

an 18-cm square brownie tin (3 cm deep), lined with greaseproof paper

Makes about 9 squares

Preheat the oven to 150°C (300°F) Gas 2.

Put the chocolate and butter in a heatproof bowl over a saucepan of barely simmering water. Do not let the base of the bowl touch the water. Stir until melted. Set aside to cool.

Put the eggs and sugar in a mixing bowl and whisk until pale and creamy. Sift in the flour and fold in gently. Fold in the molten chocolate and mix until smooth. Stir in the mixed peel and orange oil. Pour into the prepared tin and bake in the preheated oven for 15 minutes, or until slightly risen.

Leave to cool. Dust with cocoa and cut into 9 squares.

white chocolate and coffee truffle brownies

There's a little love story behind this recipe: my good friends told me on their wedding day that they used to buy each other bags of these brownies when they were courting and subsequently fell in love. I like to think that the brownies had something to do with it...

240 g dark chocolate
(at least 70% cocoa solids)

100 g unsalted butter

2 teaspoons instant coffee

3 tablespoons boiling water

3 eggs

135 g golden caster sugar

55 g plain flour

70 g white chocolate, chopped (or use chips)

cocoa powder, to dust

an 18-cm square brownie tin (3 cm deep), lined with greaseproof paper

Makes about 9 squares

Preheat the oven to 150°C (300°F) Gas 2.

Put the chocolate and butter in a heatproof bowl over a saucepan of barely simmering water. Do not let the base of the bowl touch the water. Stir until melted. Set aside to cool.

Put the instant coffee and boiling water in a cup and stir until dissolved. Set aside.

Put the eggs and sugar in a mixing bowl and whisk until pale and creamy. Stir in the coffee. Sift in the flour and fold in gently, then fold in the molten chocolate and mix until smooth. Finally, stir in the chopped chocolate.

Pour the batter into the prepared brownie tin and bake in the preheated oven for about 15 minutes. The brownies should have risen slightly.

Leave to cool completely, then dust with cocoa powder. Cut into 9 squares and serve.

popina
**savoury
straws
& bites**

gouda and hazelnut bites

Cheesy and nutty bites, great for aperitifs and parties.

140 g plain flour

70 g unsalted butter, chilled and cubed

70 g Gouda cheese, grated

1 teaspoon salt

½ teaspoon bicarbonate of soda

35 g shelled hazelnuts, roughly ground

2–3 tablespoons water

1–2 baking trays, lined with greaseproof paper

Makes about 30–40

Preheat the oven to 150°C (300°F) Gas 2.

Put the flour, butter, cheese, salt, bicarbonate of soda and hazelnuts in a food processor and pulse until the mixture resembles crumbs. Add the water and pulse until the mixture comes together into a dough.

Transfer the dough to a lightly floured surface. Roll into a log about 3 cm in diameter, wrap in clingfilm and refrigerate for about 1 hour.

Remove the dough from the fridge and unwrap it. Cut into discs about 1 cm thick. Arrange the discs on the prepared baking tray(s), spacing them slightly apart as they may spread when they are baking.

Bake in the preheated oven for about 20 minutes, or until pale gold. Remove from the oven and leave to cool. Store in an airtight container for up to 2 weeks.

stilton and celery bites

Stilton and celery are a perfect pairing. For the best result, use a strong Stilton.

140 g plain flour

60 g unsalted butter, chilled and cubed

85 g Stilton cheese

½ teaspoon salt

½ teaspoon bicarbonate of soda

1 teaspoon celery salt

2 teaspoons water

1–2 baking trays, lined with greaseproof paper

Makes about 30–40

Preheat the oven to 150°C (300°F) Gas 2.

Put the flour, butter, cheese, salt, bicarbonate of soda and celery salt in a food processor and pulse until the mixture resembles crumbs. Add the water and pulse until the mixture comes together into a dough.

Transfer the dough to a lightly floured surface. Roll into a log about 3 cm in diameter, wrap in clingfilm and refrigerate for about 1 hour.

Remove the dough from the fridge and unwrap it. Cut into discs about 1 cm thick. Arrange the discs on the prepared baking tray(s), spacing them slightly apart as they may spread when they are baking.

Bake in the preheated oven for about 20 minutes, or until pale gold. Remove from the oven and leave to cool. Store in an airtight container for up to 2 weeks.

cheshire and apple straws

The tart apple in these straws gives them a lovely sweet and sour flavour.

220 g plain flour

80 g unsalted butter, chilled and cubed

90 g Cheshire cheese, finely grated

1½ teaspoons salt

40 g Bramley or Granny Smith apple, peeled, cored and grated

1–2 baking trays, lined with greaseproof paper

Makes about 20

Preheat the oven to 170°C (325°F) Gas 3.

Put the flour, butter, cheese and salt in a food processor and pulse until the mixture resembles crumbs. Stir in the apple and bring the dough together with your hands. Add water if it's dry.

Transfer the dough to a lightly floured surface. Roll into a log about 4 cm in diameter, wrap in clingfilm and refrigerate for about 10 minutes.

Remove the dough from the fridge and unwrap it. Roll it out with a rolling pin on the work surface until about 6 mm thick, then use a sharp knife to cut the pastry into 1-cm wide straws. Twist each one before spacing them apart on the prepared baking tray(s).

Bake in the preheated oven for about 20 minutes, or until pale gold. Remove from the oven and leave to cool. Store in an airtight container for up to 2 weeks.

spinach and chilli straws

These crispy, fiery straws are to die for with a glass of cold beer and a light dip.

½ teaspoon ground coriander

½ teaspoon fennel seeds

½ teaspoon ground cumin

250 g fresh spinach (or 350 g frozen spinach, defrosted and drained)

220 g plain flour

90 g unsalted butter, chilled and cubed

1 small clove of garlic, crushed

½ teaspoon bicarbonate of soda

½ teaspoon ground turmeric

¼ teaspoon ground cayenne pepper or chilli powder

1 teaspoon salt

1–2 baking trays, lined with greaseproof paper

Makes about 20

Preheat the oven to 180°C (350°F) Gas 4.

Put the coriander, fennel seeds and cumin in a dry saucepan over medium heat and leave for a few minutes until the seeds start popping, then set aside.

Blanch the spinach in a saucepan of boiling water for 30 seconds. Drain and squeeze to get rid of excess water. Chop finely. Put all the ingredients except the spinach in a food processor and pulse until the mixture resembles crumbs. Stir in the spinach and bring the dough together with your hands. Add water if it's dry.

Transfer the dough to a lightly floured work surface and roll it out with a rolling pin until about 6 mm thick, then use a sharp knife to cut the pastry into 1-cm wide straws. Twist each one before spacing slightly apart on the prepared baking tray(s). Bake in the preheated oven for about 20 minutes, or until browned. Leave to cool. Store in an airtight container for up to 1 week.

simple spelt and oat crackers

These crackers have a deliciously mild, buttery flavour and can accompany any cheese. I recommend stronger cheese varieties like Stilton, accompanied by the Beetroot, Fennel and Apple Chutney.

210 g wholemeal spelt flour

110 g rolled oats

½ teaspoon salt

½ teaspoon bicarbonate of soda

100 g unsalted butter, chilled and cubed

80 ml water

To coat the crackers

1 egg, beaten

2 tablespoons rolled oats

1–2 baking trays, lined with greaseproof paper

Makes about 40

Put the flour, oats, salt, bicarbonate of soda and butter in a food processor and pulse until the mixture resembles crumbs. Add the water and pulse until the mixture comes together into a dough.

Transfer the dough to a lightly floured surface. Roll into a log about 5 cm in diameter, wrap in clingfilm and refrigerate for 15 minutes.

Remove the dough from the fridge and unwrap it. To coat the crackers, sprinkle the oats over a clean tray. Brush the log with the egg and roll in the oats until evenly coated. Wrap the log in clingfilm again and refrigerate for another 30 minutes.

Preheat the oven to 150°C (300°F) Gas 2.

Remove the dough from the fridge and unwrap it.

Cut into discs about 4 mm thick. Arrange the discs on the prepared baking tray(s), spacing them slightly apart as they may spread when they are baking.

Bake in the preheated oven for about 20 minutes, or until pale gold. Remove from the oven and leave to cool. Store in an airtight container for up to 2 weeks.

beetroot, fennel and apple chutney

Sweet, sour and delicately spiced, this gorgeous chutney is perfect with heavier cheeses and some of our crackers.

160 g cooked beetroot, cubed

150 g fennel, trimmed and cubed

150 g sour apple, peeled, cored and cubed

100 g red onion, cubed

190 ml spirit vinegar

220 g golden caster sugar

½ star anise

2 cloves

1 teaspoon salt

2 x 250-g jars, sterilized (see page 4)

Makes two 250-g jars

Put all the ingredients in a saucepan and bring to the boil, then cook over medium heat for 1 hour, stirring occasionally. If after 1 hour the chutney hasn't reached a jam-like consistency, leave it to cook for up to 20 more minutes.

Spoon the hot chutney into the sterilized jars and seal immediately. Leave for 2–3 days before serving. Store refrigerated for up to 2 weeks.

spinach, garlic and nutmeg muffins

250 g fresh spinach (or 350 g frozen spinach, defrosted and drained)

2 eggs

300 g plain flour

2 teaspoons baking powder

100 ml olive oil

300 ml whole milk

1 garlic clove, crushed

1 teaspoon salt

½ teaspoon crushed black pepper

½ teaspoon ground nutmeg

a muffin tray, lined with 10–12 large muffin cases

Makes 10–12

Preheat the oven to 170°C (325°F) Gas 3.

Blanch the spinach in a saucepan of boiling water for 30 seconds. Drain and squeeze to get rid of excess water. Chop finely.

Put all the ingredients, including the spinach, in a mixing bowl and mix until well combined. The batter should be quite runny.

Fill each muffin case full with batter. Bake in the preheated oven for about 25 minutes. Do not be tempted to open the oven door halfway through baking as it might cause the muffins to sink. When they are ready, they should be well risen and springy to the touch.

Muffins are always best eaten warm from the oven, but if you have some left over you can refresh them with a quick flash in the microwave. Store in airtight container for 2–3 days.

feta and tomato muffins

2 eggs

300 g plain flour

2 teaspoons baking powder

100 ml olive oil

200 ml whole milk

½ teaspoon vegetable bouillon powder (or an extra ½ teaspoon salt)

1 teaspoon salt

½ teaspoon crushed black pepper

1 small handful of fresh parsley, chopped

100 g feta cheese, crumbled

260 g cherry tomatoes, halved

a muffin tray, lined with 10–12 large muffin cases

Makes 10–12

Preheat the oven to 170°C (325°F) Gas 3.

Put the eggs, flour, baking powder, olive oil, milk, bouillon powder, salt, pepper and parsley in a mixing bowl and mix until well combined. The batter should be quite runny. Fold in the feta.

Half-fill each muffin case with batter. Pop 2 cherry tomato halves on top, then top up with batter to fill the case. Finish with another 2 tomato halves.

Bake in the preheated oven for about 25 minutes. Do not be tempted to open the oven door halfway through baking as it might cause the muffins to sink. When they are ready, they should be well risen and springy to the touch.

Muffins are always best eaten warm from the oven, but if you have some left over you can refresh them with a quick flash in the microwave. Store in airtight container for 2–3 days.

popina

savoury tarts

pastry bases

I use one of these recipes as a base for all of Popina's savoury tarts. Pizza dough works very well during the summer, while shortcrust is better suited to the wintertime. For a richer flavour and healthier choice, use wholemeal spelt to make the pizza dough, or even the shortcrust.

shortcrust

200 g strong flour

100 g unsalted butter, chilled and cubed

1 egg

½ teaspoon salt

1 tablespoon water

Makes enough to line a 23-cm tart tin

Put the flour, butter, egg, salt and water in a mixer and blitz until it forms a ball of dough. If you prefer, you can make the dough by hand, but it's easier to do this if the butter is grated or very finely chopped.

Transfer the dough to a lightly floured surface and roll with a rolling pin until 3 mm thick. Line the tart tin with the pastry and trim the excess dough neatly around the edges. Refrigerate for 20 minutes before using.

Turn to the tart recipe you are using and continue following the instructions.

pizza dough

220 g strong flour

1 teaspoon dried quick yeast

⅓ teaspoon salt

2 tablespoons olive oil

1 egg

80 ml warm water

Makes enough to line a 23-cm tart tin

Mix the flour, yeast and salt in a bowl. Make a well in the centre and pour in the oil, egg and water. Draw everything together with your hands until you get a soft dough.

Transfer the dough to a lightly floured surface and knead for a couple of minutes. The dough should be soft but not sticky. If it is sticky, add a little flour and knead again. Roll out the dough with a rolling pin until 3 mm thick.

Turn to the tart recipe you are using and continue following the instructions.

spelt pizza dough

220 g wholemeal spelt flour

1 teaspoon dried quick yeast

½ teaspoon salt

2 tablespoons olive oil

1 egg

60 ml warm water

Makes enough to line a 23-cm tart tin

Mix the flour, yeast and salt in a bowl. Make a well in the centre and pour in the oil, egg and water. Draw everything together with your hands until you get a soft dough.

Transfer the dough to a lightly floured surface and knead for a couple of minutes. The dough should be soft but not sticky. If it is sticky, add a little flour and knead again. Roll out the dough with a rolling pin until 3 mm thick.

Turn to the tart recipe you are using and continue following the instructions.

butternut squash and parmesan tart

This is a Gold Award-winning tart and has been an essential part of our autumn/winter menu for many years. Serve it as a starter or a delightful accompaniment to roast meats and red wine.

1 Spelt Pizza Dough recipe (see page 106)

1 small red onion, thinly sliced

400 g butternut squash, peeled, deseeded and cut into matchsticks

190 ml double cream

1 large egg

3 tablespoons finely grated Parmesan cheese

1 teaspoon salt

⅛ teaspoon crushed black pepper

a 23-cm loose-based fluted tart tin, greased

Makes about 8 slices

Preheat the oven to 170°C (325°F) Gas 3.

Line the tart tin with the Spelt Pizza Dough but do not trim the edges yet. Set aside.

Put the onion and butternut squash in a mixing bowl, mix and set aside.

In a separate bowl, put the cream, egg, cheese, salt and pepper and whisk well.

Pour half the cream mixture into the tart shell, then scatter the onion and butternut squash over it. Pour in the remainder of the cream mixture. Now trim the excess pizza dough neatly around the edges.

Bake in the preheated oven for 30–35 minutes, until golden. Remove from the oven and leave to cool for a few minutes. Serve warm or cold. Store refrigerated in an airtight container for up to 1 week.

goats' cheese, tomato and basil tart

With its light pizza dough base and fresh-tasting tomato, basil and goats' cheese filling, this is the perfect simple summer tart.

1 Pizza Dough recipe
(see page 106)

2 eggs

100 g Greek yoghurt

100 g strong, soft goats' cheese, mashed

1 teaspoon baking powder

50 g plain flour

1 teaspoon salt

½ teaspoon crushed black pepper

2 tablespoons finely chopped fresh basil

Topping

340 g cherry tomatoes, halved

40 g strong, soft goats' cheese, crumbled

olive oil, to drizzle

a few fresh basil leaves, to decorate

a 23-cm loose-based fluted tart tin, greased

Makes about 8 slices

Preheat the oven to 170°C (325°F) Gas 3.

Line the tart tin with the Pizza Dough but do not trim the edges yet. Set aside.

Put all the ingredients in a mixing bowl and stir well until evenly combined and a soft consistency.

Spoon the filling in the tart shell and spread evenly. For the topping, arrange the cherry tomato halves all over the filling, cut side up. Finish by scattering the goats' cheese over the top, then drizzle with olive oil. Now trim the excess pizza dough neatly around the edges.

Bake in the preheated oven for 30 minutes, or until tinged with gold. Remove from the oven, sprinkle with basil and leave to cool before serving.

aubergine, red pepper and tomato tart

This deliciously easy tart is packed full of juicy summer vegetables. It's a good choice for a sophisticated picnic with a group of friends.

1 Pizza Dough recipe (see page 106)

160 g baby aubergine, halved lengthways (or normal aubergine, chopped)

2 large red peppers, deseeded and cut into strips

1 large red onion, thinly sliced

50 ml olive oil, plus extra to drizzle

1 teaspoon salt

½ teaspoon crushed black pepper

100 g cherry tomatoes, halved

1 tablespoon freshly chopped parsley

110 g mature Cheddar, grated

150 g Greek yoghurt

a 23-cm loose-based fluted tart tin, greased

Makes about 8 slices

Preheat the oven to 180°C (350°F) Gas 4.

Put the aubergine, peppers and onion in a roasting tray (preferably non-stick), drizzle with oil, and season with the salt and pepper. Cover the tray with aluminium foil. Bake in the preheated oven for about 20 minutes, or until just soft. Remove from the oven and leave to cool, then chop the aubergine flesh (if you haven't already done so). Drain any excess juice from the roasted vegetables.

Reduce the oven temperature to 170°C (325°F) Gas 3.

Line the tart tin with the Pizza Dough but do not trim the edges yet. Set aside.

Stir the tomatoes, parsley and half the cheese into the roasted vegetables and set aside.

In a separate bowl, mix together the yoghurt and remaining cheese, then spoon into the tart shell.

Scatter the roasted vegetable mixture over the yoghurt, spreading it evenly. Now trim the excess pizza dough neatly around the edges.

Bake in the hot oven for 25–30 minutes. Remove from the oven and leave to cool.

pepper, pecorino and thyme tartlets

These light and summery tartlets are packed with vibrant red and yellow peppers, as well as gutsy Pecorino cheese and thyme. Enjoy with a glass of chilled, fruity white wine.

1 Pizza Dough recipe
(see page 106)

2 red peppers, deseeded and cut into strips

2 yellow peppers, deseeded and cut into strips

1 red onion, thinly sliced

2 tablespoons olive oil

½ teaspoon salt

½ teaspoon crushed black pepper

2 garlic cloves, crushed

½ teaspoon freshly chopped thyme

½ teaspoon freshly chopped parsley

100 g mature Cheddar, grated

80 g Pecorino cheese (50 g grated and 30 g shaved)

150 g Greek yoghurt

5 x 10-cm non-stick tartlet tins

Makes 5

Preheat the oven to 190°C (375°F) Gas 5.

In a roasting tray, mix together the peppers and onion. Drizzle with oil, season with the salt and pepper and cover the tray with aluminium foil. Roast in the preheated oven for about 20 minutes. Remove from the oven and drain any excess juice from the vegetables. Leave to cool while you line the tartlet tins.

Reduce the oven temperature to 170°C (325°F) Gas 3.

Line the tartlet tins with the Pizza Dough but do not trim the edges yet. Set aside.

Stir the garlic, thyme, parsley, 60 g of the Cheddar and the 50 g grated Pecorino into the roasted peppers and onion and set aside.

Mix together the yoghurt and the remaining Cheddar in a mixing bowl, then spoon into the tartlet shells.

Scatter the roasted pepper mixture over the yoghurt, spreading it evenly, and finish with the shaved Pecorino. Now trim the excess pizza dough neatly around the edges.

Bake in the hot oven for 25 minutes. Remove from the oven and leave to cool.

honey-roast parsnip, carrot and shallot tart

Plenty of roasted winter root vegetables with a hint of honey set in a light wholemeal spelt and olive oil pastry – this makes a great rustic starter or accompaniment to winter roasts and stews.

1 Spelt Pizza Dough recipe (see page 106)

200 g carrots, sliced on the diagonal

200 g parsnips, cut into matchsticks

180 g shallots, halved or quartered, depending on their size

1 tablespoon runny honey

40 ml olive oil

1 teaspoon salt

½ teaspoon crushed black pepper

100 g mature Cheddar, grated

150 g Greek yoghurt

a 23-cm loose-based tart tin, greased

Makes about 8 slices

Preheat the oven to 200°C (400°F) Gas 6.

Put the carrots, parsnips and shallots in a roasting tray. Add the honey, oil, salt and pepper and toss until evenly coated. Cover the tray with aluminium foil and roast in the preheated oven for 30 minutes. Remove from the oven, leave covered, and leave to cool for 10–15 minutes.

Reduce the oven temperature to 170°C (325°F) Gas 3.

Mix 60 g of the cheese into the roasted vegetables.

Line the tart tin with the Pizza Dough but do not trim the edges yet.

Mix together the yoghurt and remaining cheese in a bowl, then spoon into the tart shell.

Scatter the roasted vegetables over the yoghurt, spreading them evenly. Now trim the excess pizza dough neatly around the edges.

Bake in the hot oven for 25–30 minutes. Remove from the oven and leave to cool. Store refrigerated in an airtight container for up to 5 days.

port-poached pear, celeriac, stilton and walnut tartlets

These bites pack a real punch – strong Stilton with hints of Port, walnut and warm spices. They are ideal party canapés but I also recommend them with fine pork sausages at the Christmas dinner table.

1 Shortcrust recipe (see page 106, but use wholemeal spelt flour instead of strong flour)

1 red onion, sliced

2 tablespoons olive oil

1 tablespoon water

160 g celeriac, grated

½ teaspoon salt

½ teaspoon crushed black pepper

200 ml double cream

1 egg, beaten

100 g Stilton cheese

40 g vintage Cheddar, grated

1 teaspoon freshly chopped parsley

20 g shelled walnuts, chopped

Port-poached pears

2 firm green pears

250 ml Port

40 g golden caster sugar

1 teaspoon cloves

2 star anise

1 cinnamon stick

3 cardamom pods, bruised

12 x 5-cm loose-based fluted tartlet tins (2 cm deep), greased

Makes 12

Prepare the Port-poached pears 24 hours in advance. Peel and core the pears, then cut them into eighths. Put them in a saucepan with the Port, sugar, cloves, star anise, cinnamon and cardamom pods. Stir well and set over very low heat. Gradually bring to the boil, stirring occasionally, then cook for about 30–40 minutes. To check if they are cooked, prick them with a sharp knife – they should be soft but not falling apart. Remove from the heat and leave to cool in their cooking juices, covered, for at least 24 hours.

When you are ready to make the tartlets, make sure you have lined the tartlet tins with the Shortcrust pastry and refrigerate for 20 minutes while you make the filling.

Preheat the oven to 170°C (325°F) Gas 3.

Put the onion, oil and water in a frying pan and sauté over low heat for about 6 minutes, or until soft and the water has evaporated. Add the celeriac, salt and pepper and sauté for 5 minutes, or until the celeriac has softened. Remove from the heat and leave to cool.

Put the cream, egg and Stilton in a bowl and mix with a fork, crushing the Stilton as you go. Stir in the Cheddar and parsley and mix well. Stir into the celeriac mixture.

Remove the tartlet shells from the fridge and fill each one with the celeriac mixture. Scatter the walnuts on top. Take the poached pears out of their cooking juices and arrange 2 pieces on top of each tartlet.

Bake in the preheated oven for 20 minutes. Remove from the oven and leave to cool.

mushroom tart

If you like to pick your own mushrooms, feel free to experiment with your selection, but you can just as easily use any seasonal variety you might find at your local farmers' market.

1 Pizza Dough recipe
(see page 106)

15 g dried porcini
mushrooms

1 large red onion, cubed

2 tablespoons olive oil,
plus extra to drizzle

2 tablespoons water

1 teaspoon salt

½ teaspoon crushed black
pepper

1 teaspoon freshly chopped
thyme, plus extra whole
sprigs to decorate

2 garlic cloves, chopped

150 g button mushrooms
(halved if big)

200 g field mushrooms,
sliced about 8 mm thick

180 ml single cream

1 large egg, beaten

*a 20 x 30-cm fluted tart tin,
greased*

Makes about 6 portions

Put the porcini mushrooms in a bowl of warm water and leave to soak for 20 minutes. Drain, chop and set aside.

Preheat the oven to 200°C (400°F) Gas 6.

Put the onion, oil and water in a frying pan and sauté over low heat for about 10 minutes, or until soft and the water has evaporated. Remove from the heat and stir in the salt, pepper, thyme, garlic and porcini mushrooms. Mix well and set aside.

Put the button and field mushrooms in a roasting tray, drizzle with oil and cover the tray with aluminium foil. Roast in the preheated oven for 10 minutes. Remove from the oven and leave to cool for 10 minutes. Drain any excess juice from the mushrooms, then stir them into the onion mixture.

Reduce the oven temperature to 170°C (325°F) Gas 3.

Line the tart tin with the Pizza Dough but do not trim the edges yet.

Mix together the cream and egg in a bowl, then pour half into the tart shell. Spread the mixed vegetables over the tart, then pour in the remaining cream mixture. Now trim the excess pizza dough neatly around the edges.

Bake in the preheated oven for 25–30 minutes. Remove from the oven and leave to cool, then decorate with a few sprigs of thyme. Serve warm or cold.

roast potato and spring onion tartlets

Full of roasted new potatoes, these simple little tarts are a great accompaniment to spring lamb roasts, fish or even soups.

1 Spelt (or regular) Pizza Dough recipe (see page 106)

500 g baby new potatoes, halved

40 ml olive oil

1 ½ teaspoons salt

½ teaspoon crushed black pepper

100 g spring onions, sliced

2 garlic cloves, crushed

70 g mature Cheddar, grated

170 ml double cream

1 large egg

6 x 10-cm loose-based fluted tartlet tins, greased

Makes 6

Preheat the oven to 200°C (400°F) Gas 6.

Put the potatoes, oil, salt and pepper in a roasting tray and toss until evenly coated. Cover the tray with aluminium foil and roast in the preheated oven for 20 minutes. Remove from the oven and leave to cool for about 10 minutes.

Reduce the oven temperature to 170°C (325°F) Gas 3.

Stir the spring onions, garlic and cheese into the roasted potatoes and mix well.

Line the tartlet tins with the Pizza Dough but do not trim the edges yet.

Mix together the cream and egg in a bowl, then divide half between the tartlet shells. Spread the vegetables over the tartlets, then pour in the remaining cream mixture. Now trim the excess pizza dough neatly around the edges.

Bake in the hot oven for 25 minutes, or until the filling looks golden. Remove from the oven and leave to cool for 5 minutes, then serve warm.

spinach, feta and tomato quiche

Creamy with a generous amount of spinach and sweet cherry tomatoes.

1 Shortcrust recipe (see page 106)

200 g fresh spinach (or 320 g frozen spinach, defrosted and drained)

60 g feta cheese, crumbled

1 garlic clove, crushed

½ teaspoon salt

½ teaspoon crushed black pepper

2 large eggs, beaten

200 ml double cream

90 ml semi-skimmed milk

60 g cherry tomatoes, halved

a 23-cm loose-based fluted tart tin, greased

Makes 6 slices

Preheat the oven to 170°C (325°F) Gas 3.

Make sure you have lined the tart tin with the Shortcrust pastry and refrigerate for 20 minutes while you make the filling.

Blanch the spinach in a saucepan of boiling water for 30 seconds. Drain and squeeze to get rid of excess water. Chop finely, then put in a mixing bowl with the feta, garlic, salt and pepper and mix well.

In a separate bowl, mix the eggs, cream and milk, then pour half of it into the tart shell. Scatter the spinach mixture over the top and spread evenly, then pour over the remaining cream mixture. Arrange the tomato halves over the top, cut side up.

Bake in the preheated oven for 30 minutes. Remove from the oven and leave to cool before serving.

leek and mature cheddar mini quiches

So simple and yet so delicious; I suggest using strong mature Cheddar and fresh young leeks when they are in season.

1 Shortcrust recipe (see page 106)

2 large eggs, beaten

190 ml double cream

50 ml semi-skimmed milk

100 g mature Cheddar, grated

1 small leek, thinly sliced

½ teaspoon salt

½ teaspoon crushed black pepper

6 x 10-cm loose-based fluted tartlet tins, greased

Makes 6

Preheat the oven to 170°C (325°F) Gas 3.

Make sure you have lined the tartlet tins with the Shortcrust pastry and refrigerate for 20 minutes while you make the filling.

Put the eggs, cream and milk in a bowl and mix well, then stir in the cheese, leek, salt and pepper.

Remove the tartlet shells from the fridge and fill each one with the leek mixture.

Bake in the preheated oven for 30 minutes. Remove from the oven and leave to cool before serving. Store refrigerated in an airtight container for up to 1 week.

courgette and fennel tart

Fresh and summery, serve this with a rocket salad, fish and white wine.

1 Pizza Dough recipe (see page 106)

350 g courgettes, sliced 1 cm thick

200 g fennel, trimmed and sliced 1 cm thick

1 small red onion, sliced 5 mm thick

40 ml olive oil

1 teaspoon salt

½ teaspoon crushed black pepper

1 tablespoon freshly chopped parsley

100 g mature Cheddar, grated

150 g Greek yoghurt

a 10 x 33-cm tart tin, greased

Makes about 6 portions

Preheat the oven to 200°C (400°F) Gas 6.

Put the courgettes, fennel, onion, oil, salt and pepper in a roasting tray and toss until evenly combined. Cover the tray with aluminium foil. Roast in the preheated oven for 30 minutes. Remove from the oven, leave covered, and leave to cool for 10–15 minutes.

Reduce the oven temperature to 170°C (325°F) Gas 3.

Drain any excess juice from the vegetables, then mix in the parsley and 60 g of the cheese. Line the tart tin with the Pizza Dough but do not trim the edges yet.

Mix the yoghurt and remaining cheese in a bowl, then pour into the tart shell. Scatter the roasted vegetables over the top, spreading them evenly. Now trim the excess pizza dough neatly around the edges. Bake in the hot oven for 25–30 minutes. Remove from the oven and leave to cool.

See photographs on pages 128 and 129.

cheese burek

This wonderful Serbian speciality is taken from my mother Rozalia's collection of recipes and I have reworked it in two versions. It is easy to make and always impresses dinner guests. I recommend using strong, barrel-aged feta cheese for the filling if you can get it.

250 g cottage cheese

60 g barrel-aged feta cheese, crumbled

190 g reduced-fat Greek yoghurt

2 eggs, beaten

2 tablespoons olive oil, plus extra to brush

½ teaspoon bicarbonate of soda

1 ½ teaspoons salt

6 large sheets of thick filo pastry (47 x 32 cm, see Note below)

a 20-cm springform tin (7 cm deep), base-lined with greaseproof paper

Makes 6 slices

Preheat the oven to 180°C (350°F) Gas 4.

Put the cottage cheese, feta, yoghurt, eggs, oil, bicarbonate of soda and salt in a mixing bowl and mix well.

Make sure you have plenty of space to work on. Take one filo sheet and lay it on the work surface. Lightly brush it all over with oil. Place a second filo sheet on top. Spoon one-third of the cheese mixture on to the filo and spread it evenly across the surface, leaving the very edges clear.

Fold over each short side by 2 cm. Do the same with a long side, then carry on rolling it downwards (not too tightly) until you've rolled all the filo and made a tube. Gently lift up the tube and curl around the inside edge of the cake tin. The filo tears easily so try to lift it gently, but don't worry too much if it tears a little.

Repeat this entire process with the remaining filo sheets, making 2 more tubes and fitting them end to end in the tin until you have a spiral. Brush the top with oil.

Bake in the preheated oven for 40 minutes until deep golden and risen. Don't worry if parts of the pastry look a little burnt – this tastes great! Remove from the oven and leave to cool for a few minutes. It freezes well – defrost and warm up in the oven before serving.

Note: The large sheets of filo pastry can be found in Middle Eastern shops or the freezer aisle of supermarkets. I just let it defrost for 1 hour before I start. If you can't find such large sheets, simply overlap your sheets to make the correct size and remember that you'll need more to begin with.

spinach and cheese burek

I have been making this recipe for many years and it sells like hotcakes on my market stalls. Traditionally, in parts of Eastern Europe, burek is enjoyed with a glass of keffir, a type of drinking yoghurt.

300 g fresh spinach
(or 420 g frozen spinach,
defrosted and drained)

110 g cottage cheese

100 g Greek yoghurt

1 large egg, beaten

30 ml olive oil, plus extra
to brush

30 ml sparkling water

½ teaspoon bicarbonate
of soda

1 teaspoon salt

250 g large filo pastry sheets

*an 18-cm square brownie tin
(4 cm deep), greased*

Makes 4–6 portions

Preheat the oven to 180°C (350°F) Gas 4.

Blanch the spinach in a saucepan of boiling water for 30 seconds. Drain and squeeze to get rid of excess water. Chop finely, then put in a mixing bowl with the cottage cheese, yoghurt, egg, oil, water, bicarbonate of soda and salt and mix well.

Lay a filo sheet in the base of the brownie tin, leaving the excess pastry hanging over one side of the tin. Brush with oil. Lay another sheet on top so that the overhang is on the opposite side of the tin. Spread a generous tablespoon of spinach mixture over the filo sheet. Lay another 2 sheets over the filling and scrunch up the excess pastry to fit the tin. Brush with oil. Spread another generous tablespoon of spinach mixture over the filo sheet. Lay another 2 sheets over the filling and scrunch up the excess pastry to fit the tin. Brush with oil. Keep going until you've used up the spinach mixture. You should end with a layer of filling.

Finally, fold over the overhanging pastry to cover the top of the burek and brush all over with more oil. If the top isn't entirely covered with pastry, add another sheet and brush with oil.

Bake in the preheated oven for 40 minutes until deep golden and risen. Remove from the oven and leave to cool for a few minutes. It freezes well – defrost and warm up in the oven before serving.

smokey vegetable, butter bean and paprika filo strudels

You can use different kind of beans for this recipe: as well as butter beans, pinto, flageolet and haricot are excellent too. I recommend serving this filo strudel with salads, soups or a few slices of good cured chorizo.

50 ml olive oil

1 small red onion, chopped

160 g red and/or yellow peppers, deseeded and cubed

100 g aubergine, cubed

100 g courgette, cubed

230 g tinned butter beans, drained and rinsed

½ teaspoon smoked paprika

1 teaspoon salt

⅓ teaspoon crushed black pepper

1 garlic clove, crushed

2 small tomatoes, chopped

2 eggs, beaten

6 large sheets of thick filo pastry (47 x 32 cm, see Note below)

a baking tray, greased

Makes 2 – serves about 10

Preheat the oven to 180°C (350°F) Gas 4.

Heat 2 tablespoons of the oil in a frying pan and sauté the onion over medium heat for about 5 minutes. Add the peppers and sauté for 5 minutes. Add the aubergine, courgette, beans, paprika, salt and pepper and cook for a further 10–15 minutes until the aubergine and courgette have softened. Remove from the heat and leave to cool for 15 minutes. Stir in the garlic, tomatoes and eggs.

Make sure you have plenty of space to work on. Take one filo sheet and lay it on the work surface. Lightly brush it all over with oil. Place a second filo sheet on top. Lightly brush it all over with oil. Repeat with a third sheet.

Divide the vegetable mixture in half and spoon one half along one longer side of the filo sheets, leaving a 2-cm gap on either side and spreading the filling about 5 cm wide. Fold the longer side of the pastry, nearest the filling, about 2 cm in, then roll the filo pastry up, tucking in the sides as you go. Brush the top of the strudel with a little more oil.

Repeat the entire process with the remaining filo sheets to make a second strudel. Place both on the baking tray.

Bake in the preheated oven for 25 minutes. The strudels should be pale gold. Remove from the oven and leave to cool for 5 minutes.

Note: The large sheets of filo pastry can be found in Middle Eastern shops or the freezer aisle of supermarkets. I just let it defrost for 1 hour before I start. If you can't find such large sheets, simply overlap your sheets to make the correct size and remember that you'll need more to begin with.

little margherita pizzas with olives

Imagine a bright summer's day, an alfresco lunch, chilled white wine, good company and a leisurely afternoon ahead. The only thing missing is these little pizzas. Alternatively, it's Saturday afternoon on a chilly winter's day and you have no plans for the evening. Make up some of these, crack open a good bottle of red and settle down on the sofa in front of a movie.

First phase dough

200 ml warm water

1½ teaspoons dried quick yeast

130 g strong flour

Second phase dough

1 tablespoon olive oil

1½ teaspoons salt

165 g strong flour

Topping

250 ml passata

2 tablespoons olive oil, plus extra to brush

1 tablespoon freshly chopped oregano, plus extra to decorate

½ teaspoon salt

¼ teaspoon crushed black pepper

150 g mozzarella cheese, torn into pieces

40 g stoned black olives, chopped

2–3 non-stick baking trays

Makes 16

To make the first phase dough, put the warm water and yeast in a mixing bowl and whisk, then add the flour and whisk again until well mixed. Cover and set aside in a warm place for 1 hour.

In the meantime, make the topping. Put the passata, oil, oregano, salt and pepper in a bowl, mix and set aside.

After 1 hour the first phase dough will be bubbly and have increased in size. For the second phase, add the oil, salt and flour and mix well to form a dough. Transfer to a well floured surface and knead well for a few minutes. Divide the dough into 16 and roll each into a ball. Roll out with a rolling pin until you have a base about 10 cm in diameter. Put the bases on the baking trays and brush well with oil. Spread some of the tomato sauce over each base and top with mozzarella and olives. Leave to rest in a warm place for about 30 minutes.

Preheat the oven to 200°C (400°F) Gas 6.

Bake in the preheated oven for about 12 minutes. Remove from the oven and scatter more oregano over the top. Leave to cool for a couple of minutes, then serve hot.

rustic focaccia with red pepper and onion

Light and simple, this flavoursome bread is great with soups and a tasty addition to your picnic basket.

2 teaspoons dried quick yeast

250 ml warm water

390 g strong flour

1 teaspoon dried basil

3 tablespoons olive oil

1½ teaspoons salt

Topping

50 ml olive oil

½ red pepper, deseeded and thinly sliced

½ red onion, thinly sliced

a 20 x 30-cm baking tray or tart tin, greased

Makes 8–10 portions

Put the yeast in a jug, then slowly whisk in the warm water and set aside for 5 minutes.

Put the flour, basil, oil and salt in a mixing bowl and mix. Add the yeast mixture and mix well until you get a smooth dough. Transfer to a well floured surface and knead for a couple of minutes. The dough should be soft but not sticky. If it is sticky, add a little flour and knead again. Return the dough to the mixing bowl, cover and leave to prove for 1 hour in a warm place. The dough should increase significantly in size.

Uncover your mixing bowl and transfer the ball of dough to the well floured surface. Knead well for a couple of minutes, then leave to rest for 5 minutes.

Roll out the dough with a rolling pin until big enough to fit your baking tray. Transfer to the baking tray and stretch it to fit snugly. Push your finger into the dough repeatedly to make dents about 2 cm apart all over the surface.

For the topping, drizzle the oil evenly over the focaccia and scatter the pepper and onion over the top. Cover and leave to rest for another 40 minutes. It will increase in size again.

Preheat the oven to 200°C (400°F) Gas 6.

Uncover the focaccia and bake in the preheated oven for 15 minutes – it should be pale gold. Remove from the oven and leave to cool. Store in an airtight container or bread bag for up to 2 days.

mini cornbreads with vegetables

These delicious and versatile little breads have a lovely light texture. They make great accompaniments to soups, salads, dips or heavier roast meats. They are so good you could have them any time: breakfast, lunch or dinner.

1 egg, separated

260 ml skimmed milk

200 ml vegetable oil

120 g strong flour

160 g polenta (fine cornmeal)

1 teaspoon baking powder

1 teaspoon salt

1 large red pepper, deseeded and thinly sliced

9 cherry tomatoes, quartered

6 x 10-cm loose-based fluted tartlet tins, greased

Makes 6

Put the egg yolk, milk, oil, flour, polenta, baking powder and salt in a mixing bowl and whisk well until smooth. Refrigerate for 30 minutes to allow the polenta to soak up the liquid. This makes for better cornbread.

Preheat the oven to 200°C (400°F) Gas 6.

Remove the cornbread batter from the fridge. Put the egg white in a separate, grease-free bowl and whisk until it forms stiff peaks, then fold it gently into the batter. Spoon the batter into the tartlet tins almost to the top and scatter the pepper and tomatoes on top.

Bake in the preheated oven for 15 minutes. Remove from the oven and leave to cool before serving warm. Store in an airtight container for up to 3 days.

index

acknowledgements

I'd like to thank the following people:

My friend and business partner Matt Gruninger for his dedication and support; all past and present Popina kitchen and market staff and drivers for their hard and dedicated work without whom Popina would not be here; Sergei Strelets and Laura Amos for their inspiration and hard work; in the office, Milena Velgosova and Karolina Wojtun; in the kitchen, Raphal Lukanski, Tibi Tehel, Magda Wozniak, Joanna Kawalerczyk, Tibor Varga, Bela Nagy, Graciano Vaz-Andrade, Kingsley Uyigue, Zsuzsanna Bimbo, Arthur Dzuiba, Tomasz Dyczko; Marion Gough for believing in us; Francesca Shepherd for all her help and work on PR; Igor Jocić for all Popina designs and his generous help over the years; Jose Lasheras for all Popina's own photographs; Johnny at The Print Factory for never letting us down; Patrick Cairns for his helping hand; all my friends who generously helped me in those first difficult years and throughout – Clare Pearson, Nick Henderson, Melissa Odabash, Jorge Camman, Tim Sanderson, Ryan Board, Susan Hicks, Hackney Business Venture for the initial grant and Mr Jonathan Miller at Fortnum & Mason who was the first buyer to notice Popina and who very kindly offered his helping hand. For their support and fine quotes, thank you to Elizabeth Hurley, William Sitwell, Editor of *Waitrose Food Illustrated*, Jenni Muir of *Time Out* and Henrietta Green for her help and support over the years and for a lovely foreword. Thanks to Mark Handley and Cheryl Cohen from London Farmers Markets; Portobello Road Market Office; Louise Brewood from Broadway Market; to everybody at Ryland Peters & Small, in particular Alison Starling, Céline Hughes and Steve Painter; book photographer Peter Cassidy; food stylist Linda Tubby; Jane Milton for testing recipes; to all our distributors and suppliers over the years and to all the fabulous Popina customers for their support and dedication; to my husband and my family. And last but not least, thank you to The Prince's Trust and His Royal Highness The Prince of Wales for the personal interest he has taken in Popina.